Date Due

MAR 9 '80			
AUG 4 1992			

Portraits and Personalities

An Introduction to the World's Great Art

Portraits and Personalities

AN INTRODUCTION TO THE WORLD'S GREAT ART

LUISE C. KAINZ

Chairman of Art, Washington Irving High School, The City of New York

OLIVE L. RILEY

Director of Art, Board of Education, The City of New York

HARRY N. ABRAMS, INC. *Publishers* NEW YORK

CONTENTS

PLATE 1. The Painter in His Studio. *Jan Vermeer (Dutch, 1632-1675).*
Oil on canvas. Kunsthistorisches Museum, Vienna, Austria

PLATE 2. Siddhartha in Meditation. *Chinese, Northern Wei Dynasty, 286-534* A.D.
Limestone carving from the Lung-Men caves. The Museum of Fine Arts, Boston, Mass.

1

Early Image Makers

WHAT IS PERSONALITY? How does it differ from character? Perhaps we can clarify the difference by saying that personality is the outer evidence of one's character. The qualities that make up character are within the person, while the personality is that which is seen by the world.

The artist has the gift of seeing both the outer and the inner man. His eye discerns the personality; his penetrating mind is sensitive to those inner qualities that are hidden from most of us. Although each individual is different, there are certain universal qualities that belong to all mankind. In line, form, and color, the artist captures both the significant differences that mark the individual and the human qualities that we share in common. Thus the artist can represent individuals, great and small, each with his own personal traits and qualities, yet each with something that we recognize as universally human.

If we study carefully the portraits that follow, we shall come to know and to understand people from many ages and lands. We shall also see the familiar qualities that are brought to life by the artist. Each portrait will have significance, not only because each person is unique, but also because each artist's interpretation of his subject is his own.

EGYPTIAN PORTRAITS

Early forms of portraiture were unlike those we know today. Artists drew, painted, and modeled ideal representations of men and women, usually rulers, or gods appearing in human form. What the artist strove to capture was a de-

PLATE 3. Queen Nefertiti. *Egyptian, Eighteenth Dynasty.*
Painted limestone. State Museums, West Berlin, Germany

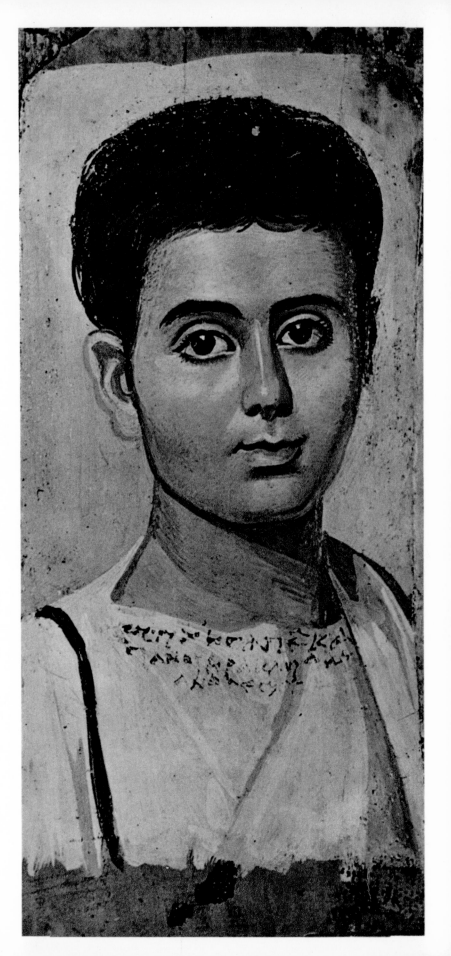

PLATE 4. Portrait of a Boy. *Egypto-Roman, from the Faiyum, Lower Egypt, 2nd century* A.D. *Encaustic painting on wood. The Metropolitan Museum of Art, New York, N.Y. (Gift of Edward S. Harkness, 1918)*

gree of likeness within an impressive image of those qualities that made his subject famous and revered. Royalty, dignity, or spiritual power, for example, could be made clear to all in some visual form. Concepts of mightiness, both mental and physical, were embodied in a human form which bore the name and symbol of the person or divine being in whose honor the painting or statue was made. Such portraits may be thought of as "type portraits." At their best they are deeply impressive, since they embody the finest qualities attributed to a ruler or his gods.

Queen Nefertiti (Plate 3), made about 1360 B.C., shows the wife of an Egyptian ruler of the New Empire as unmistakably queenly. The perfection of her flawlessly carved features, and the calculated balance of an imposing headdress worn with dignity and ease, establish an image of royalty. As characterized by the Egyptian sculptor, the queen appears aloof, more god-like than human.

Portrait of a Boy (Plate 4), painted in Egypt during the second century A.D., shows a more realistic approach to portraiture. It was then customary, after wrapping mummies in linen, to insert their painted portraits on the panel of the mummy case. These portraits are true works of art, for they reveal an expression of deep emotion. The large, sad eyes seem suitable to the funeral portrait, yet the realism of expression makes this boy as familiar to us as the boy next door.

GREEK PORTRAITS

Greek art contributed to this change from the formalized likeness to the more human likeness. The importance of the ancient Greeks in world civilization lies in their creation of a new way of thinking about mankind in relation to the universe. This is clearly seen in their art. Their gods and goddesses were represented as superb creatures. The Greek ideal was to strive for a combination of moral and physical beauty and to represent it in all their sculpture.

Thus the supreme expression of the Greek spirit is seen in *Athena Lemnia* (Plate 6), thought to be a copy of a bronze by Phidias, a famous Greek sculptor. She has a serenity that is untouched by earthly cares, yet she is the personification of intelligence and the idealism of the human spirit. A mathematical perfection of proportion was carefully worked out by the sculptor so that every part of the human figure would be in correct relation to the whole, thus insuring perfect balance and perfect form. This was the Greek way of creating

beauty. Together with a philosophy of pure reasoning and thinking, it consti-
tutes what to this day is considered the classic form of Greek thought and art.

Comparing *Athena Lemnia* with the Greek *Portrait Head* (Plate 5)
made in the early part of the first century B.C., we sense even more clearly the
trend toward the revelation of the personal and human aspects of a subject.
The *Portrait Head* shows us someone who is far from being physically and
intellectually perfect. One is conscious of an ordinary man whose worries
and uncertainties are clearly and skillfully reflected in his countenance.

CHINESE SCULPTURE

Chinese art was concerned with the Buddhist religion after its introduction into China during the first century of the Christian era. *Siddhartha in
Meditation* (Plate 2) originated in China during a period known as the
Northern Wei Dynasty, which lasted approximately from the third to the
sixth century A.D. In this relief sculpture one again sees the use of the human
figure to suggest a spiritual concept, with this difference, however: the figure
remains human, rather than becoming so completely idealized. Prince Siddhartha was an Indian who founded Buddhism in China. He is known to have
left his family and to have lived in poverty in order to teach the concepts of
the Buddhist religion. The easy and relaxed pose of his figure and the almost
informally carved details of his garment leave our eyes free to search for the
message he bears. One can sense a "divine" being who is aware of the human
weaknesses of his followers, yet embraces them with gentle, universal love.

BYZANTINE ART

With the decline of the Roman Empire in the fourth century A.D., the
Emperor Constantine moved the capital from Rome to Byzantium, which
was then renamed Constantinople. Today we know this city as Istanbul. Since
Christianity had become the Roman state religion, church building flourished,
as did many other forms of art. Byzantine art reveals a fusion of Greek and
Roman influences and the Oriental art of the Eastern world. It has been called
the Christian art of the East.

Although controversies later banned image making from time to time,
under Constantine master artists took over the decoration of the magnificent

13

PLATE 5. Portrait Head. *Greek, about 80 B.C., Delos, Greece. Bronze. National Museum, Athens, Greece*

PLATE 6. Athena Lemnia. *Roman marble copy after bronze original of about 450 B.C. by Phidias. Museo Civico, Bologna, Italy*

14

PLATE 7. Empress Theodora and Her Attendants. *Byzantine, about 547* A.D.
Mosaic. Church of San Vitale, Ravenna, Italy

churches that were being built. Mosaics were a prevailing form of decoration since they were particularly suited to the architectural design and needs of the times.

Mosaic decorations were carried out by means of small pieces of colored glass or stone, set one by one in moist plaster. The nature of mosaic lends itself to the formal rather than the realistic qualities of that art. Among the many beautiful examples of Byzantine art after Constantine is the mosaic decoration *Empress Theodora and Her Attendants* (Plate 7). Here you see the Empress and four of her retinue. The artist had no intention of making portraits or characteristic representations of the persons in this group. The solemn, almost

15

motionless figures are dominated, because of her central position and size, by the majestic Theodora. Her striking gown and elaborate headdress proclaim her queenly rank, while the halo behind her head suggests that she also has an aspect of divinity. The contoured figures confront us squarely; their expressions have an intensity that is created by their large, dark, and clearly marked eyes. Richly patterned garments have a wealth of detail for us to enjoy.

The background of this mosaic adds greatly to the color movements to be found throughout the scene. There are both vertical and horizontal areas that reinforce the symbolic message. Glass backed with gold leaf in portions of the background suggests heavenly space, while the canopylike shape is suggestive of regal power.

In studying this impressive mosaic, we are amazed at the ability of the artist to triumph over the difficulties of executing a complicated design with tiny pieces of colored glass and stone, and achieve such a monumental work of art.

2

Mighty Men of the Renaissance

IN THE WESTERN WORLD during the first thousand years of the Christian era, artists were in the service of the Church. Their murals and mosaics were entirely devoted to church decoration and religious teaching. In their paintings, the human figure was treated in a symbolic, or conventional, manner.

By the end of the thirteenth and the beginning of the fourteenth century in Italy, certain highly talented artists, such as Giotto, the Florentine painter, and Duccio, the Sienese painter, among others, expanded the scope of painting in ways hitherto unknown. The influence of a new personal outlook inspired artists to portray the Madonna and the saints as living people capable of human emotions such as tenderness, sympathy, and humility. Then, too, these pioneer painters sometimes placed their subjects in a convincing, three-dimensional world rather than using only the traditional background of flat color or gold used by earlier artists. Furthermore, these subjects were painted so that they appear to have weight and solidity. Giotto's innovations, especially, heralded new ideas that inspired succeeding generations of painters.

During the fifteenth century, significant changes occurred in the artists' choice of subject matter. While they continued with religious painting and sculpture, they also began to portray people as individuals in their own right. From Flanders, France, and Italy came paintings that foretold a whole new world of artistic thought and accomplishment. By the early fifteenth century, Italy, a leader in the new movement, had already moved toward the flowering of the Renaissance.

The Renaissance spirit was born of a search for new knowledge. It was an age distinguished by explorers, inventors, poets, scholars, philosophers,

PLATE 8. Self-Portrait.
*Leonardo da Vinci
(Italian, 1452-1519).
Drawing, red chalk.
The Royal Library, Turin, Italy*

PLATE 9. Mona Lisa.
*Leonardo da Vinci
(Italian, 1452-1519).
Oil on canvas.
The Louvre, Paris, France*

and artists who were gifted with remarkable creative and intellectual powers. The overwhelming desire to enliven all forms of art with a new spirit of knowledge and vision broke through the hard and fast rules that had dominated art. Man felt impelled to reach for new horizons. Returning to the Greek philosophers who held man as the "measure of all things," the Italians welcomed the "renaissance," the "rebirth" (for that is what the word Renaissance means), of the power of the human mind and will to set its own goals and to determine its own destiny.

Exploration in the sciences and intellectual curiosity about all phases of human life had a direct effect on the artists of that time. The application of knowledge, the study of mathematics, science, and anatomy, brought new ideas and new enthusiasms to artists. In this period the artist emerged as an independent, creative person who was capable of asserting his individuality through his art.

By the sixteenth century, Renaissance painting had reached such astounding heights that it is now known as the "Golden Age of Painting."

LEONARDO DA VINCI

This famous artist is a perfect example of the Renaissance spirit. Gifted with a broader range of creative power than that possessed by any previous artist, Leonardo became a pioneer in many fields of endeavor. His studies of the natural sciences—botany, geology, and zoology—recorded in careful drawings in his notebooks astonish us with their clarity and vision. His treatise on the art of painting reveals how clearly the artist's eye could probe both the outer appearance and the inner structure of natural forms.

Physical and mechanical sciences also fascinated Leonardo, leading him to design experimental models of all kinds—airplanes, armored tanks, submarines, and even a revolving stage. Gifted in music as well, this versatile artist could sing admirably, accompany himself on a lute, and improvise music and verse at will. His *Self-Portrait* (Plate 8) reveals both his sensitivity and his intelligence.

When Leonardo was thirteen years of age, he became an apprentice in the studio of a famous artist, Verrocchio. A youthful prodigy, the boy devoted himself to the study of anatomy by dissecting dead bodies and by constantly drawing people, as well as other forms of nature. The new studies of perspective and of light and shade also engaged his attention. As he grew older he became interested in architecture, sculpture, metalwork, and in many other allied arts, so it was inevitable that he produced comparatively few paintings.

Leonardo's portrait of *Mona Lisa* (Plate 9) has provoked romantic speculation because of her elusive personality as he shows it. The meaning of her smile, her challenging gaze, and her relaxed hands never fail to attract and hold attention. Although he worked for many years on this portrait, the artist considered it unfinished. To us who see it today, it seems to be complete and marvelously alive, a painting in which all parts, background as well as figure, are completely unified. Mellow colors, diffused light, hazy shapes and tones create a dreamlike atmosphere, one that enfolds the solidly modeled figure and the carefully constructed landscape. This portrait is more than the presentation of an interesting personality; it reveals the artist's remarkable power to vitalize his subject and to create a living legend for all time.

A search for essential qualities in the human personality may be felt in Leonardo's *Madonna, Child, St. Anne, and Infant John the Baptist* (Plate 10). Since this drawing, or "cartoon," as it was then called, is one of several made in preparation for a painting, the artist did not finish it in detail. Essentially the drawing suggests how the figures might be compactly grouped and what

PLATE 10. Madonna, Child, St. Anne, and Infant John the Baptist. *Leonardo da Vinci (Italian, 1452-1519). Drawing, black chalk heightened with white. The National Gallery, London, England*

PLATE 11. Portrait of Michelangelo. *Giorgio Vasari (Italian, 1511-1574). Fresco. Palazzo della Cancelleria, Rome, Italy*

21

poses might best suggest the individual emotions or thoughts of each person. Notice how the Child is brought out by the movements and glances of the other three figures. Modeling of forms is accomplished through a subtle shading of light tones into darker tones. The artist's tremendous interest in compositional arrangement is combined with his intense feeling for the emotional and spiritual meaning of his subject. Grace and dignity are blended with warm and loving human qualities.

MICHELANGELO

Michelangelo Buonarroti, often called "The Titan," is a pre-eminent example of a dynamic and forceful personality in art. Since this world-famous Florentine artist lived until the age of eighty-nine, his life span covered the period of the Renaissance at its height. At that time, Italian cities competed with one another to produce outstanding monuments of art. Ruling families and churchmen sought out the most famous artists to create masterpieces for them. Michelangelo, considered to be a genius even during his lifetime, was constantly urged to accept important commissions, often of huge proportions. A rugged individualist, he consistently displayed an amazing independence toward the wishes of his influential clients. The *Portrait of Michelangelo* (Plate 11) painted by Vasari, an artist and writer who knew him well, suggests that he was strong-willed, as indeed he was described by his biographers.

Michelangelo's life is the dramatic story of a genius. After a brief apprenticeship at the age of thirteen under Ghirlandajo, a Florentine fresco painter, he became a protégé of Lorenzo de' Medici. This ruler, known as Lorenzo the Magnificent, had established an academy for young sculptors. It was there that Michelangelo learned the art of stone carving. The first of his major sculptures, a *Pietà*, brought him great acclaim. He eventually became one of the world's greatest sculptors, perhaps the greatest of all.

At one time Michelangelo competed with Leonardo da Vinci, each of them sketching the plan for a large fresco for the Council Hall of his native Florence. Then, called to Rome, he somewhat unwillingly undertook a commission from Pope Julius II to paint the ceiling of the Sistine Chapel in the Vatican, the residence of the Popes. For four arduous years, stretched on a scaffold, Michelangelo painted directly on the ceiling. He covered its extensive area with over three hundred figures that magnificently depict the creation and the downfall of mankind. In later years, this titanic artist painted a

PLATE 12. Jeremiah. *Michelangelo Buonarroti (Italian, 1475-1564).*
Fresco. Sistine Chapel, The Vatican, Rome, Italy

scene of the Last Judgment on the altar wall of the chapel. The vigorous grandeur of Michelangelo's paintings will long continue to attract countless admirers to view them.

The painting of the prophet *Jeremiah* (Plate 12), to be seen between two arches on the ceiling of the Sistine Chapel, shows the striking power and dramatic expressiveness that Michelangelo could impart to each figure he painted. His interpretation of the Old Testament prophet may truly be called a creation, for the combined qualities of Jeremiah's body and spirit are so forcefully and clearly brought out. The monumental figure seems lost in deep, brooding thought, yet in viewing the scenes of mankind caught up in earth's turmoil, Jeremiah is shown as one who views human beings with compassion rather than with indignation or wrath.

RAPHAEL

The third and youngest Florentine artist of the Renaissance to be hailed in his own time as a genius was Raphael Sanzio, a younger contemporary of Leonardo da Vinci and Michelangelo. As may be seen in his *Self-Portrait* (Plate 13), Raphael was gentle in nature and boyish in appearance. In accordance with the practice of training artists at an early age, he became a pupil of Perugino, a painter of religious subjects. By the time Raphael was in his early twenties, he was a recognized and admired artist. Until his death at the age of thirty-seven, he lacked neither influential friends nor money to be spent on luxurious living.

Although Raphael is considered to be a less versatile master than Leonardo or Michelangelo, since he lacked their vast originality, his talents are recognized as far above those of his predecessors and contemporaries. He was a superb draftsman and an adept worker. His popular Madonnas, for which he received great acclaim, set standards for similar religious paintings that have survived to this day. Perhaps less widely known are the large and dramatic murals that he painted on the walls of certain rooms in the Vatican. His penetrating portraits are considered to be among his best works.

Raphael's triple portrait painting, *Pope Leo X with Cardinals Giulio de' Medici and Luigi de' Rossi* (Plate 14), is one of the finest of its kind. The Pope's dominating figure shows us that Raphael scorned to flatter his subject, as many portrait painters feel they must do. Dignified and clearly seen as a man of authority and intelligence, the churchman is brought out by the light that emphasizes the rich color and texture of his garments. Each of the two cardinals also has a personality of his own. Notice that they are painted in a half-light so that they will not detract from the main subject of the painting. It is interesting to study the bell, book, and handsome magnifying glass in the sharply focused foreground. They are rendered with cameralike fidelity, perhaps to symbolize Pope Leo's scholarly mind.

TITIAN

Tiziano Vecelli, known as Titian, was the most famous of the sixteenth-century High Renaissance artists who brought fame to Venetian painting. In contrast to Michelangelo, who at this time was engaged in a wide variety of activities involving painting, architecture, and sculpture, Titian devoted his life entirely to painting. His production was vast. According to legend, he

PLATE 13. Self-Portrait. *Raphael Sanzio (Italian, 1483-1520). Drawing, silverpoint. The Ashmolean Museum, Oxford, England*

25

PLATE 14. Pope Leo X with Cardinals Giulio de' Medici and Luigi de' Rossi. *Raphael Sanzio (Italian, 1483-1520). Oil on wood. The Uffizi Gallery, Florence, Italy*

PLATE 15. Portrait of a Man. *Titian (Tiziano Vecelli, Italian, 1477? [more probably about 1490]-1576). Oil on canvas. The National Gallery, London, England*

painted a picture a month for more than eighty years, and remained active until his ninety-ninth year. His *Self-Portrait* (Plate 16), painted in his later years, suggests the nervous energy and forcefulness of a dedicated artist.

Titian, as official painter of Venice, decorated many churches and produced countless religious paintings. He is best known today, however, for the amazing vitality of his portraits. It is easy to understand why this prolific artist was the most eagerly sought-after portrait painter of his time. He treated his subjects almost tenderly and with great sympathy. As Titian recorded their personalities, it was always the best, the most favorable, and most interesting aspect that he chose to present to the viewer. Then, too, he had supreme technical skill. Working directly with oil paint on canvas, Titian captured a likeness without apparent effort. A master of highlights and shadows, of transparent and opaque color, he could enhance the surfaces of his paintings with textural qualities more brilliant and lifelike than the actual materials he portrayed.

Portrait of a Man (Plate 15) was made when Titian was still a young man. The subject, said to be a friend of the artist, is directly and convincingly presented. His striking costume gives force and solidity to the portrait. Richly textured and colorful, the bulky garment with its sweeping lines leads our eyes to his clearly defined face.

3

Windows on the World

THE SPIRIT OF THE Renaissance was felt not only in Italy but in northern countries as well. In that part of Flanders which today is called Belgium, certain of the fifteenth- and sixteenth-century painters were also explorers in a sense, for they sought to reveal the human rather than the purely spiritual aspects of life. These artists discovered the beauty of the natural world—not only the world of people, but also the visual beauty in which they lived.

JAN VAN EYCK

The study of physical life, combined with worldly knowledge, is apparent in the work of Jan van Eyck, a fifteenth-century painter who is considered the first important Flemish artist and the forerunner of other fine Flemish artists to come. *Giovanni Arnolfini and His Bride* (Plate 17) actually portrays a solemn wedding ceremony that took place in the home and was witnessed by the painter, as seen in his own inscription above the mirror, "Jan van Eyck was here." Each item, painted with the same exquisite care as the two figures themselves, has a special meaning in this painting. They are not merely details, but symbols that have long been forgotten. Standing in their stocking feet, the bride and groom have cast off their slippers because they are on holy ground; the mirror signifies purity; one burning candle was customary when taking a vow; the dog represents faithfulness in marriage. We can see how skillful Van Eyck was in recording the effects of the elements of light, space, and atmosphere on the figures and on their surroundings. Notice how

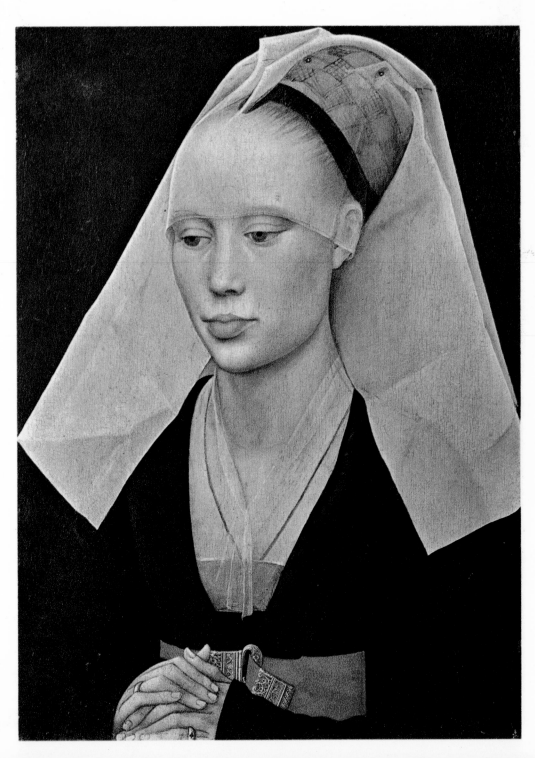

light intensifies their heads and hands; how subtly it brings out their tiny figures reflected in the mirror on the back wall; how it flickers about the room and suggests the textures of the well-polished chandelier, the rich fabric of the wedding costumes, and the silkiness of the little dog's coat of hair.

In this painting Van Eyck not only shows us the physical appearance of his subjects, but their characters as well. Giovanni, or John, is solemn, dignified, and rather forbidding; his wife is timid and apparently shy.

During his lifetime, Van Eyck also helped to develop a new technique of painting in oil on wood that eventually brought about the wide use of oil paint on canvas. A superb craftsman as well as a sensitive painter, he made a notable contribution to the art of painting.

ROGIER VAN DER WEYDEN

The important cycle of Flemish painting that began with Jan van Eyck received further impetus from another genius, Rogier van der Weyden. Facts related to his early years and training are somewhat uncertain. Over a lifetime of painting, he produced a number of religious works, for which he is renowned. Van der Weyden was one of the finest portrait painters of all time, and although his portraits are few in number they greatly influenced the portrait painters of other European countries.

Portrait of a Lady (Plate 18) clearly indicates both his style and his concern with the character of his subject. Her clearly patterned face and headdress create strong shapes, yet the modeling of her features is restrained and almost shadowless. Color is subdued and delicate, except for the sparkling red of her belt. The artist's brushwork is highly refined. The lady, thought to be the daughter of a duke, is interpreted by the artist as a withdrawn person, more conscious of her inner thoughts and feelings than she is of the outer world. Her downcast eyes evade the artist's glance. The visual description of her face has been simplified to emphasize her character as it was felt and seen by the artist. The high forehead usually associated with the intellectual person has been emphasized, as are the long-fingered and tightly clasped hands.

ALBRECHT DURER

During the late fifteenth and early sixteenth centuries, at the time when the Italian Renaissance masters were bringing the art of painting to new

PLATE 19. Self-Portrait
Albrecht Dürer (German, 1471-1528).
Drawing, silverpoint.
The Albertina, Vienna, Austria

PLATE 20. Study of an Old Man.
Albrecht Dürer (German, 1471-1528).
Drawing, brush and ink.
The Albertina, Vienna, Austria

33

1493 Mein sach die gat / Als es oben schtat

PLATE 21. Self-Portrait. *Albrecht Dürer (German, 1471-1528). Oil on canvas. The Louvre, Paris, France*

PLATE 22. A Prince of Saxony. *Lucas Cranach the Elder (German, 1472-1553). Mixed media on wood. The National Gallery of Art, Washington, D.C. (Ralph and Mary Booth Collection)*

heights of glory, and when the Flemish painters were beginning their exploration of man and his world, a similar spirit of investigation flourished throughout the northern countries of Europe. New studies in scientific perspective and in the proportions of the human figure aroused the interest and curiosity of artists to such an extent that many of them wished to have a firsthand acquaintance with these discoveries.

Albrecht Dürer was the greatest of the German artists who traveled to Italy in search of knowledge. This artist had an unusually broad background for his times. Trained through a three-year apprenticeship in metalwork, printmaking, and painting, and equally proficient in mathematics, he also wrote and published books on human proportions, the teaching of measurements, and the art of fortifications. Dürer's originality and vigor, together with an intense feeling for the beauties of nature, no matter how small and delicate, characterized all his early work. Leonardo's investigations of the structural beauty of the human figure and the peaceful serenity of his paintings, as well as the works of other Italian masters, greatly impressed Dürer and were reflected in his work.

Today we are accustomed to the idea that artists often make self-portraits. It is interesting to realize, however, that Dürer was the first artist who, throughout his lifetime, made a series of self-portraits. The first record we have of him as an artist is a self-portrait made at the age of thirteen (Plate 19). The precision and delicacy of this silverpoint drawing foretell his future greatness. His inquiring and keenly observant eye, and his constant and restless search for essential truths, may be discovered in all of his later self-portraits. His first painting of himself is shown in Plate 21. We see Dürer as a young man who is wearing, quite casually, the elaborate costume of his time. One does not, however, receive the impression that the artist wishes to make himself appear attractive or even handsome. With eyes peering searchingly into a mirror, he carefully recorded what he saw. Notice how certain elements in the painting have been either stressed or subdued. The nose, for example, sharply accentuated, becomes the dominant feature of his face. The texture of his hair and the gathers of his shirt are only lightly suggested. The dark background serves as an excellent foil for the light tones of flesh and shirt, and for the varied reds and greens that are repeated throughout the painting. In this portrait Dürer reveals the man he was known to be, a man of remarkable power, conviction, and sincerity.

Dürer's superb draftsmanship is brilliantly illustrated in his *Study of an Old Man* (Plate 20). This drawing shows us the infinitely complicated forms that the artist must study before he can hope to paint them. Dürer's love of minute detail and his accurate rendering of it bring fresh insight to the art of portraiture. His drawing of the old man shows an intense feeling for the beauty of an aged, careworn face. The deep contemplation that is often the result of an unusually long life is suggested with vividness and sympathy.

LUCAS CRANACH THE ELDER

Lucas Cranach, another German painter, was a contemporary of Albrecht Dürer. As a court painter, he was one of many famous artists who were called upon to make portraits of members of highly placed families. Although he was expected to please his patrons, Cranach, like Dürer, did not believe in making his subjects more attractive than they actually were. He remained loyal to his belief in the ultimate importance of a portrait as a work of art and exerted every effort to use all his talent for drawing, color, and design to reveal his subject's true appearance and personality.

In *A Prince of Saxony* (Plate 22), we see precise and clear drawing of the boy's features: eyes, nose, and mouth are brought out with the utmost simplicity. Cranach's sensitive, unbroken line produces an expression of calmness and serenity in his subject. What thoughts lie hidden under the soft, smooth surface of this young face? The large eyes looking out on the world show trust and hope. A delicate yet firmly drawn mouth, almost smiling, and rounded cheeks give an impression of a spirited youngster, even though he is formally dressed in brocade and satin and his movements are restricted by a high-collared garment and a jeweled crown. The light tones of the hair and the shape of the face against the dark background make a most effective design. The reappearance of the light tones in the hand helps to unify the painting.

HANS HOLBEIN THE YOUNGER

Holbein, also a German painter and a contemporary of Dürer and Cranach, was renowned before he was twenty years of age. His reputation as a portrait painter became more and more firmly established over the years. During the later part of his life he settled in England, as court painter to King Henry VIII, and his services were eagerly sought by royalty and other wealthy patrons. It would seem, from the number of portraits that Holbein produced during this time, that he painted every important person in England.

PLATE 23. Anne of Cleves. *Hans Holbein the Younger (German, about 1497-1543). Tempera and oil on parchment. The Louvre, Paris, France*

PLATE 24. Portrait of Francis I. *Jean Clouet (French, about 1486-1541). Tempera and oil on wood. The Louvre, Paris, France*

After the death of Jane Seymour, Queen of England, Holbein was sent abroad to paint the portrait of a possible new wife for the king. It was at this time that he painted *Anne of Cleves* (Plate 23). It is recorded in history that Henry VIII was so taken with Holbein's painting of this German noblewoman that he married her.

In painting her portrait, Holbein was expected to satisfy certain requirements and demands. Anne of Cleves most assuredly wished to be shown to full advantage. She would expect every jewel and elegant detail of her lavish costume to be carefully represented. Her demands could have been successfully met only by an artist of Holbein's stature. In spite of the countless details he included in *Anne of Cleves*, there is still a magnificent simplicity in the entire painting. The clear line movement of the drapery, the simple masses of an expressionless face and placid hands, and the striking silhouette of the entire figure against the dark background build a solid composition in which details do not intrude, but take their place in the total arrangement.

One can also see that Holbein made no effort to represent the future queen as a beautiful woman. She appears, as she undoubtedly was, a plain, rather lifeless person, endowed only with the enduring magic wrought by a magnificent portrait painter.

JEAN CLOUET

The role of court painter did not originate with Holbein, even though his fame rests chiefly on his accomplishments in this difficult field of painting. In the sixteenth century in France, for example, there were a number of noted artists working under the patronage of King Francis I. While Jean Clouet, his court painter, was a contemporary of Holbein, and his *Portrait of Francis I* (Plate 24) has certain similarities to *Anne of Cleves*, there is no evidence that one painter was influenced by the other's work.

The similarities that you will first notice are the bulky figures that fill most of the picture area, the straightforward gazes, and the brilliantly detailed costumes. The flashiness of the King's costume, however, is more pronounced. If it were not for the strength of personality suggested by the dynamic head with its sharply drawn features, and by the elegantly assured hands, the costume and background might well have overwhelmed the sitter.

4

New Master Artists

AFTER THE REFORMATION in the early sixteenth century, the painting of religious subjects was frowned upon in the Protestant countries. By the end of the century the northern provinces of the Netherlands had broken away from Spain and become an independent, Protestant-ruled country, which we now know as the Netherlands or Holland. The southern provinces, which roughly correspond to modern Belgium, remained loyal to the Spanish crown. We call the artists from this area Flemish artists, because the most important of these provinces was Flanders. While Flemish artists continued to be patronized by the court and the Church, Dutch artists turned to the middle classes for patronage.

PETER PAUL RUBENS

In Flanders, some two hundred years after Van Eyck, Peter Paul Rubens came into prominence. This seventeenth-century artist had a long, highly successful, and fashionable career. He was extraordinarily favored in many ways. Unusually intelligent, Rubens learned to speak seven languages while still quite young. A professional painter at twenty-one, he was considered the most promising artist of Flanders. When he was twenty-three years of age, he traveled from Antwerp to Venice on horseback, was received by royalty, and became an eager student of the great Renaissance masters. After eight years' travel in Italy and Spain, Rubens returned to Antwerp, where he was named court painter by Archduke Albert, the Spanish regent of Flanders.

PLATE 25. Rubens and Isabella Brant. *Peter Paul Rubens (Flemish, 1577-1640). Oil on canvas. Pinakothek, Munich, Germany*

PLATE 26. The Artist's Sons, Albert and Nicholas. *Peter Paul Rubens (Flemish, 1577-1640). Oil on wood. Collection Prince Liechtenstein, Vaduz, Liechtenstein*

43

All that Rubens learned from his studies and travels became part of his personal style. His mastery of fluid brushwork has never been surpassed. His paintings are always identified by brilliant flesh tones and luminous colors. Whether he was painting religious or mythological subjects, or those concerned with the lives of his countrymen, Rubens' work had an immense vitality and power, as did the artist himself. It is said that he started to work at daybreak and worked steadily throughout the day during his entire lifetime. Actually, as his services came to be more and more in demand, Rubens employed many assistants to help him complete the more than three thousand paintings commissioned from him.

To celebrate his wedding to Isabella Brant, a beautiful girl of eighteen, Rubens painted himself sitting hand in hand with his young bride (Plate 25). The formal and elaborate dress of the period in no way detracts from the grace and beauty of the wearers. In fact, the movements of their figures and the harmoniously repeated sweep and swirl of their costumes establish the dynamic line scheme known as the S curve, for which Rubens is famous. Notice how this line scheme unites the two appealing figures. Continuous movements lock them in a solidly structured unit, so that we feel them to be a young couple rather than two separate personalities.

Rubens' painting *The Artist's Sons, Albert and Nicholas* (Plate 26) reveals his warm affection for these two young boys. At first glance we are naturally drawn to a study of their elegant costumes. It is obvious that they have been dressed in their best finery for this important occasion. Further study of the painting brings us an awareness of the astute way in which each boy was posed. Albert, somewhat self-conscious, is standing in the studied attitude of a stylish young man of his time. The book he is holding suggests that he, the son of a well-to-do artist, is being properly educated. An arm casually placed around the shoulders of his young brother reveals Albert's brotherly affection. Young Nicholas appears to be a sturdy, independent boy. In a natural, childlike way, he seems to be more interested in watching a bird which is fluttering at the end of a string than he is in having his portrait painted.

Although all of Rubens' large paintings are filled with figures in dramatic action and motion, according to a style called Baroque, his portraits are more intimate and reveal the deeper feelings of his subjects. These portraits bear out contemporary descriptions of him as a quiet, agreeable, and devoted painter who is quoted as having said as a young boy, "I had rather be an artist than a king."

FRANS HALS

Frans Hals was the most popular portrait painter of the town of Haarlem, in Holland. A man of abundant vitality, he loved all the gay aspects of life; his enjoyment of them is reflected in his paintings. In *Yonker Ramp and His Sweetheart* (Plate 27), the infectious qualities of laughter and high spirits are brilliantly conveyed. Two healthy, happy people are shown in a tavern scene. The effect is one of a fleeting impression. Within the next second, one feels, the young couple will change in pose and expression—the man's upraised arm holding the wineglass may be lowered and the couple may embrace one another. Hals's brilliant brush strokes seem to have been set down at great speed. They are as spirited as the subjects themselves. Although we are impressed by their look of great spontaneity, the poses of the young Dutch cavalier and his sweetheart, their expressions and gestures, and the artist's deft use of color were all carefully calculated. The painting probably took many hours to complete. Hals's strong and direct application of paint was a departure from the smoothly blended surfaces that had characterized Van Eyck and other early painters. His technique points in the direction of the French Impressionists, whose work you will see in Chapter 6.

WILLIAM HOGARTH

Frans Hals and other Dutch artists established a tradition of informality in portraiture. About one hundred years after Hals, we find this tradition carried forward in the work of William Hogarth, a famous English painter. Rejecting the currently fashionable portrait, with its formulas of pose and prettiness, he focused his attention upon the contemporary scene and the earthy atmosphere of town fairs, taverns, and fish markets. *The Shrimp Girl* (Plate 28) is one of his most famous works of art. As in Frans Hals's paintings, we find broad brush strokes capturing a warm and high-spirited personality. With what seems to be effortless painting, Hogarth conveyed his admiration for the vitality and native charm of his subject.

At an early age Hogarth had trained his "mind's eye," as he called it, to retain his impressions of the people and scenes that delighted him. Unlike Frans Hals, who had posed his models carefully for *Yonker Ramp and His Sweetheart,* Hogarth did not need a model to recall the healthy young woman to whom he had been attracted.

PLATE 27. Yonker Ramp and His Sweetheart. *Frans Hals (Dutch, 1580-1666).*
Oil on canvas. The Metropolitan Museum of Art, New York, N.Y.

PLATE 28. The Shrimp Girl. *William Hogarth (English, 1697-1764).*
Oil on canvas. The National Gallery, London, England

REMBRANDT VAN RIJN

Almost three hundred years have passed since Rembrandt's death, yet today the personalities he created in his paintings speak to us with ever-increasing strength, spirit, and conviction. He was a true genius; his work is not only the chief glory of Dutch painting, but also places him as one of the most important artists of all time.

Born in Leyden, Holland, at the beginning of the seventeenth century, Rembrandt gave up his university studies to become an artist. Quite rapidly he found himself to be a sought-after portrait painter, acquired a well-to-do bride, and developed a taste for luxurious living. He continued, however, to be a prolific worker. The death of his wife and reversals of fortune undermined his financial position, yet, as an artist, he steadily progressed in his power to interpret human beings in broad, universal terms.

The fame of Rembrandt's group paintings that include portraits, such as *The Night Watch* and *The Anatomy Lesson of Dr. Tulp,* is widespread. It is through a study of Rembrandt's superb portraits of individuals, however, that we can intimately examine his amazing strength as an artist. No matter how often we see them, there is always something new and inspiring that speaks directly to us.

We become very conscious of Rembrandt's characteristic style of painting when we study his searching *Self-Portrait* (Plate 29), one of sixty self-portraits that he made during his lifetime. Here we see the artist as an aging man whose countenance forcefully displays his troubled mind and his keenly sensitive, highly trained eye and hand. His image, as he saw it in a mirror, was placed on canvas with all the sincerity this great artist had at his command.

Our first impression of Rembrandt's *Portrait of a Rabbi* (Frontispiece) and of *Titus Reading* (Plate 30) is of their brilliantly lifelike, glowing qualities. Then the dramatic lights and deep shadows, always associated with Rembrandt, attract our attention. But his achievements are not restricted to the magic realism with which his brush reproduces the textures of flesh, hair, and cloth. His brush strokes create vivid personalities that appear and disappear in light that is now brilliant, now diffused. His exhaustive use of a few limited colors creates a strong impact and produces a complete unity of drawing, light and dark tones, and color. And above all, there is the emotional and spiritual quality of his own personality as it emerges from his paintings.

Portrait of a Rabbi is a study of a man who befriended Rembrandt in his later, poverty-stricken years. We are brought into direct visual contact with a personality so moving and challenging that we are almost forced to speculate as to what manner of man he was, what he thought, and how he acted. The dark color scheme is a wonderful foil for the few areas of bright color that so brilliantly accentuate the rabbi's expressive features.

In the portrait of Titus, who was Rembrandt's beloved son, there is utter peace and calm. We enter into the quiet mood of this painting and feel as though we were sitting beside the young reader and enjoying the book with him. The magic glow of golden color, which only Rembrandt could produce, along with the blending of rich olive greens and brownish blacks, continues to attract our eyes long after the initial enjoyment has passed. The play of light on Titus's face comes from no particular single source. It produces a feeling of movement in the boy's expression and in his lightly painted hair. Notice how thoughtfully Rembrandt planned the brilliant light in the left-hand corner of the painting. It brings out the shape of the hat and flickers over important parts of the head, the figure, and the book. All this movement of light contributes to the mood and atmosphere of the painting and helps us concentrate on the serene and sensitive head of Titus.

JAN VERMEER

Rembrandt's genius has sometimes seemed to outshine that of his contemporaries. Many other Dutch painters among those known as the "Little Masters" were also greatly gifted. Jan Vermeer was one of these artists. His paintings have their own highly personal style and quality. They are serene and orderly, balanced and harmonious, timeless as art itself.

The Painter in His Studio (Plate 1) establishes the mood of the artist. It is one of quiet concentration. The scene is so convincingly presented that one feels that the onlooker, rather than the painter himself, is standing on the threshold of the studio.

Vermeer's extraordinary skill in capturing the way in which light from a particular source envelops objects in space may remind you of Van Eyck's similar interest in capturing "reality." Turn for a moment to Plate 17 to discover what the work of these two artists has in common.

The smallness of both paintings and their numerous details make them intimate pictures. Similar subjects were produced in great quantity for the small, rather dark homes of the Dutch people. For us today, they make vivid the moods of the family life of their time.

PLATE 30. Titus Reading. *Rembrandt van Rijn (Dutch, 1606-1669).*
Oil on canvas. Kunsthistorisches Museum, Vienna, Austria

5

Mysticism and Realism

SPAIN WAS SO DEEPLY TORN by religious and cultural conflicts that its art—
painting, sculpture, and the allied arts—did not flourish during the Renaissance centuries as they did in Italy. The final conquest of the Moors in 1492,
under Ferdinand and Isabella, was the culmination of a long struggle.

Yet during the fourteenth and fifteenth centuries there did develop an
art that reflected a recognizably Spanish spirit and way of life, one that was
deeply concerned with religion. Naturally, Spanish painting reflects to a
greater or lesser degree the vitality of Italian and Flemish painting, since
many artists traveled freely from country to country and to some extent were
influenced by foreign contacts and foreign accomplishments.

EL GRECO

El Greco, the first of the great Spanish painters, was a Greek who was
born on the island of Crete. Like many artists of his time, Domenicos Theoto-
copoulos, better known as El Greco ("The Greek"), made his way to Venice
and worked with Titian and other Venetian masters. After studying the works
of other famous artists—Michelangelo and Raphael, for example—he went to
Spain and eventually settled in Toledo for the remainder of his life. There
he worked continuously for almost forty years.

A presumed self-portrait of El Greco (Plate 31) shows his unmistakable
individuality. Physically he appears to be an elderly and tired man, yet his
force of character is apparent. We sense that he was intelligent and cultured,

somewhat withdrawn, yet possessed of great inner power. In this portrait you will notice the distortion of natural appearances that is strongly characteristic of El Greco's style. Elongation, or lengthening the human figure, in this case the head and its various features, adds a certain emotional intensity to his self-portrait.

The oval of the narrow head, noticeably repeated in the eyes, in the ears, and in the shape of the ornamental ruff, all contribute to an impression of deep contemplation and concern with the mystical rather than the practical aspects of life. El Greco's searching and imaginative vision has transferred his self-portrait from a mirrored physical likeness into an interpretive study of a remarkable personality.

You will notice in studying this portrait that El Greco used a very limited palette of colors. Perhaps he thought that a wide color range would distract us and prevent concentrating on the personal qualities he wished to reveal.

El Greco's highly individual style of painting is evident and recognizable in all his work. It establishes him as one of the most fascinating painters of all time. Interesting to note, however, is the fact that he did not attain widespread success in his lifetime. Not until the late nineteenth century was his work fully appreciated by "modern" artists and writers who recognized him as a master painter.

The portrait of *Fray Felix Hortensio Paravicino* (Plate 32) introduces us to a man who was a famed poet and scholar as well as a monk. It is another typical example of the intense way in which El Greco viewed his subjects. Color tones, ranging from deep, greenish black to delicate whites and flesh tones, bring out the monk's face dramatically. His scholarly and religious character is shown clearly through the way in which the artist painted the refined features and the direct and steady gaze. The pose of the figure and the delicate way in which the books are held clarify for us the essential nature of the devout poet. The character of El Greco's brushwork is unmistakable. It contributes greatly to the painter's success in going far beyond the external appearance of his subject in order to probe the complex fabric of his being.

DIEGO VELAZQUEZ

El Greco's theories of perspective and color were handed down to Velázquez by the teacher to whom he was apprenticed as a young art student.

PLATE 31. Probable Self-Portrait. *El Greco (Spanish, 1541-1614).*
Oil on canvas. The Metropolitan Museum of Art, New York, N.Y.

PLATE 32. Fray Felix Hortensio Paravicino. *El Greco (Spanish,*
1541-1614). Oil on canvas. Museum of Fine Arts, Boston, Mass.

At the age of nineteen he was recognized as a talented young artist, at twenty-four he was appointed court painter to King Philip IV of Spain. While this position restrained his freedom to some extent, and brought him only a modest living, his art nevertheless flourished.

Although Velázquez was familiar with the mystic qualities of El Greco's works, he preferred to paint only what was clearly visible. He was a realist in the best sense of the word, as was Vermeer (see Plate 1); his paintings rest on a firm basis of truth to nature. Direct observation of his subjects and the effects of the light, shadow, space, and atmosphere that encompassed them are forcefully and harmoniously recorded.

Technically, Velázquez was a master painter, the greatest of the seventeenth-century Spanish artists. His brushwork was so masterful and so assured that its perfection is not immediately apparent. Many artists who followed him strove to match the unassuming certainty of his painting techniques. In later years, the Impressionist painters found Velázquez' way of using paint and brush a valuable source of study for a means of capturing the effects of light and atmosphere.

Velázquez found an occasional release from the burden of painting formal portraits of royalty—he painted forty of the king himself—by painting a subject for his own pleasure. Toward the end of his career he painted *The Maids of Honor* (Plate 33), which shows us how happily he departed from the standards set for court portraits.

Let us study first the highly original and involved placing of many figures within a spacious area. Think of yourself as standing on the threshold of a room in a palace. You are facing the central figure, the charming Infanta Margarita, who is posing for her portrait. She is attended by her two maids of honor, a guardian dog, and a merry little dwarf. Velázquez himself, standing before a huge canvas on which he is painting, pauses to look directly out of the picture. Possibly he sees the king and queen, whose reflections appear in the mirror on the distant wall, and who are watching as he paints their little daughter. The apparently casual arrangement of this composition, as you now can see, is actually one that is highly organized. The edge of the tall canvas, for example, gives scale to the people in the scene and also emphasizes the importance of the painter himself. The geometric structure of receding lines of perspective gives depth and space to the entire painting.

The serenity of the scene is reinforced by Velázquez' realization of the important role that light and shadow play in creating atmosphere, and by the sensation of momentarily arrested movement that is conveyed. The little figure of the princess stands out beautifully. As our eyes move back into the painting we are led, by diminishing lights and increasing shadows, to the background where the other people—almost like actors on a stage—play their lesser roles.

A detail of *The Maids of Honor* (Plate 34) gives us further opportunity for studying Velázquez' painting techniques more closely and of seeing how each brush stroke helps to form the expression, the shape, and the textural surface of the child's head. *The Maids of Honor* is generally thought to be the artist's masterpiece.

JEAN-BAPTISTE CHARDIN

Among the eighteenth-century artists in France, we find one who especially represents a transition between traditional and new ideas in painting. Jean-Baptiste Chardin was the child of poor parents, and he was self-taught as an artist. Modest and unassuming in character, his work reflects the beauty he found in ordinary people and their surroundings. His approach to painting, unlike that of several of his contemporaries, was sober and thoughtful rather than spontaneous.

Chardin had much in common with Vermeer, the Dutch painter whose work you have seen in *The Painter in His Studio* (Plate 1). Both artists had a comfortable, middle-class interest in ordinary people seen in everyday surroundings and in daily activities. However, you may have noticed that Vermeer's figures are apt to seem very carefully posed, while Chardin's subjects seem to be quite unaware that they are being painted.

The House of Cards (Plate 36) reveals Chardin's powers of observation as well as his discrimination in presenting his subject. By reducing the figure of the young man to its simplest and most essential forms, and by relating the movements of his figure to those of the table and its contents, Chardin presents a well-ordered scene, one that is arranged with flawless taste. Just as Vermeer was interested in the effects of color, light, and atmosphere, so Chardin in this painting shows his interest in creating a mood, and his concern with subtle color qualities. These qualities mark him as an artist who is approaching the discovery of a new, wider role for color in painting.

PLATE 33. The Maids of Honor. *Diego Velázquez (Spanish, 1599-1660).*
Oil on canvas. The Prado, Madrid, Spain

PLATE 34. The Maids of Honor *(detail of Plate 33).*

PLATE 35. Mrs. Freake and Baby Mary. *Unknown artist (American, seventeenth century). Oil on canvas. The Worcester Museum, Worcester, Mass. (Gift of Mr. and Mrs. Albert W. Rice)*

GILBERT STUART

The art of painting did not develop in America until the eighteenth century. Earlier painters were actually untrained, although many of them were excellent craftsmen. Known as limners, they were adept at decorating carriages, houses, and painting signs for shops and taverns. During this time, the Colonies gradually became more and more prosperous and worldly. Well-established gentlemen searched for a "face painter" to record for posterity the appearance and existence of members of their families, since those were the days before the camera had been invented. Many of the early portraits made at this time followed formulas, since the limner was more craftsman than artist. Bodies often seem to be made of wood, and faces appear characterless. Yet certain of these early painters, many of whose names are unknown today, produced portraits that reveal an unmistakable, though untrained, talent.

One of the best-known paintings by an American "primitive" painter is *Mrs. Freake and Baby Mary* (Plate 35). Notice how the unknown artist shows his feeling for the human appeal of his subject. Mother and child form a compact group, yet each figure is well brought out. As with the best of the American primitive paintings, there is a naïve charm that delights the viewer.

By the middle of the eighteenth century, Colonial portrait painting began to reach the standards set by European countries. Young American painters went to England for the training they could not obtain in their own country. Among them was Gilbert Stuart, now considered the finest portrait painter of his day. In his youth Stuart showed considerable talent, and by the age of fourteen he had many commissions to paint portraits. As a young man he studied in England to develop craftsmanship in the use of oil paint and the placing of highlights and shadows on the faces of his subjects to make them appear more lifelike. His own keen insight helped him to produce countless portraits that are remarkable for their sensitivity and perception.

After Stuart's return to America he became famous for the many portraits he painted of George Washington. However, a more important legacy is to be found in those of his portraits that reveal his understanding of human nature. *Mrs. Richard Yates* (Plate 37) is considered to be one of the finest American portraits. Stuart's decisive characterization of this New England woman makes her seem extraordinarily vital. Her Puritanical strain is tempered by intellect and elegance. Her self-assurance is apparent in the pose of her hands. The glow of life shines through this portrait.

PLATE 37. Mrs. Richard Yates. *Gilbert Stuart (American, 1755-1828).*
Oil on canvas. The National Gallery of Art, Washington, D.C.
(Andrew Mellon Collection)

6

Color Comes to Life

ART IS NEVER AT A STANDSTILL. An urge for personal expression always prompts artists to search out new ways to make old subjects fresh, vital, and in keeping with the times. Every period in history has its own quality, as do the people who shape and mold it to their taste. Outward and inward changes taking place in men's lives are reflected in their thinking and in their modes of expression as well. The very word "movement," so vital to all life, is also used to denote a particular style or new direction in the world of art. To look back over hundreds of years is the best way to survey the new developments that we now classify as movements or styles.

After the great Renaissance period that left its impact on artists of many nations, there was a gradual decline in art quality. Eighteenth-century artists, still using the old techniques, lost strength and vitality of interpretation and became superficial or even frivolous. Their attitudes reflected their particular period. The nineteenth century, however, brought about radical changes in the thinking and attitude of people toward many problems. With a new emphasis on the human value of all people and on their daily lives, great changes occurred. These are seen in the way that artists reacted to what they observed.

FRANCISCO GOYA

While El Greco and Velázquez may be considered Late Renaissance or Baroque artists, Goya's art belongs specifically to the late eighteenth and

64

early nineteenth centuries. This notable painter and graphic artist ushers in a new era in Spanish painting, one in which an expanded freedom in personal expression is clearly apparent.

When he was a boy, Goya constantly made vivid sketches of his neighbors. The power and somewhat fantastic quality of his youthful drawings brought him to the attention of interested patrons. At the age of fifteen, they arranged that he enter an artist's studio to receive his first formal instruction in art. An excitable young man, he brought a tremendous vitality to his painting, as well as to his experiments in etching and lithography. In both the fields of painting and graphic arts, Goya became well known as a promising young artist.

When Goya was in sympathy with his subjects, he gave full rein to his innate love of humanity. The portrait *Don Manuel Osorio de Zuñiga* (Plate 38) shows the painter's affection for this little boy. Goya surrounded him with his favorite companions: three cats, a pet crow, and caged songbirds. The child's large, dark eyes command attention, as do his dark hair and the red suit with its elegant satin and lace trimmings. Notice the play of light on the upper part of the child's figure. Let your eye travel down to the shadowed area in the lower left-hand corner of the painting, where the drama of playful crow and fascinated cats is masterfully enacted. The portrait of Don Manuel is ranked as one of the truly great portraits of children. Its vivid colors are, in a sense, typical of Goya's own lively, colorful personality.

At the age of sixty-nine, Goya painted a revealing *Self-Portrait in a Tall Hat* (Plate 39). Notice the dashing, broad way in which he worked. Goya did not spend long hours making preliminary sketches of his models—in this case himself—but worked directly on canvas, blocking in important shapes with color, and working in detail only when he was satisfied that the likeness was truly expressive of the subject's human qualities. In this self-portrait, Goya presented himself as tolerant and benign, a person who could be amusing and easily amused. His personality is subtly suggested in the quality of his brush strokes and in the shapes and textures of his face and costume.

JEAN-AUGUSTE-DOMINIQUE INGRES

In the early nineteenth century in France there were strongly entrenched schools of painting, among them the Academic, the Classical, and the Romantic schools. Many painters were involved with biblical, mythologi-

L S. D. MANVEL OSORIO MANRRIQVE DE ZVÑIGA S DIGNOR NACIO ENA ABRIL

PLATE 38. Don Manuel Osorio de Zuñiga. *Francisco Goya (Spanish, 1746-1828). Oil on canvas. The Metropolitan Museum of Art, New York, N.Y.*

PLATE 39. Self-portrait in a Tall Hat. *Francisco Goya (Spanish, 1746-1828). Oil on canvas. Kunsthistorisches Museum, Vienna, Austria*

PLATE 40. The Guillon-Lethière Family. *Jean-Auguste-Dominique Ingres (French, 1780-1867). Drawing, pencil. Museum of Fine Arts, Boston, Mass.*

cal, classical, or romantic subjects, rather than with the contemporary scene. Interestingly enough, one of these painters, who considered himself devoted to the classic concept of ideal beauty, was one of the most observant portrait artists of all times. While Jean-Auguste-Dominique Ingres held color in low esteem, he valued draftsmanship above all other attributes of the artist. The basis of art, he felt, was the line that clearly revealed or suggested physical form.

Ingres's penetrating eye, insight, and remarkable draftsmanship brought him many clients. In *The Guillon-Lethière Family* (Plate 40) one finds a masterfully drawn and charmingly presented family portrait group. There is no need for color to suggest the structure and solidity of each characteristically posed figure. The vitality of the drawing acquaints us, almost personally, with the proud parents and their child.

EDOUARD MANET

Although he lived more than two hundred years after Velázquez, Manet found much to inspire him in the work of this Spanish artist. Freeing himself from the restrained, formal, and rather cold painting of his immediate predecessors in France, Manet introduced a refreshing realism into his work. Some art historians consider him to be the first modern painter, for he broke away from the prevailing rules of subject matter and composition. Manet's early painting, *Boy with Cherries* (Plate 41), reveals his initial interest in capturing what to him were the all-important qualities of color and light. The model for the painting, a young errand boy, does not seem posed for the occasion, although actually he was. Casually leaning over a well, he is boldly and perfectly placed within the picture frame. A highly effective play of reds against greens, and the flat, almost shadowless treatment of his figure show that Manet relied on differences of color, rather than on varying shades of light and dark, to obtain his easy, natural effects. In this painting Manet set down what you, as a viewer, might have caught at first glance: accents of bright color and an impression of gaiety and laughter.

In comparing Chardin's *The House of Cards* (Plate 36) with Manet's *Boy with Cherries*, there are certain similarities that you can easily discover. One might, however, note the different way in which the near jacket sleeve of each boy was painted. Manet has recorded the effect of light on a color and has shown how it differs from the same color when seen in shadow, while Chardin shows less concern for the effects of light and shadow and has painted more of the "local color," or true color, of an object.

Manet and certain other artists of his time developed a theory related to the direct painting of a visual image. What they saw, rather than what they

PLATE 41. Boy with Cherries.
Édouard Manet (French, 1832-1883).
Oil on canvas. Calouste Gulbenkian
Foundation, Lisbon, Portugal

PLATE 42. A Bar at the Folies-Bergère. *Édouard Manet (French, 1832-1883).*
Oil on canvas. The Courtauld Institute of Art, London, England

PLATE 43. The Glass of Absinthe. *Edgar Degas (French, 1834-1917).*
Oil on canvas. The Louvre, Paris, France

knew or remembered, became the basis of their art. The critics of the time, disturbed by this revolutionary approach to painting, called this movement "Impressionism." Since Manet and the other Impressionists were departing from traditional ways of working, each one had to rely on his individual inventiveness, imagination, and feeling to guide him. Exploration into new subject matter and painting techniques took several of them far afield of traditional artists, and this brought them adverse criticism. Today they are accepted as forerunners of modern art and admired for accomplishing so much in establishing new forms of personal expression.

While *Boy with Cherries* shows Manet's early interest in using color to record a fleeting glance, one of his last works, *A Bar at the Folies-Bergère* (Plate 42), shows a subject that is complex in color treatment. It includes both directly seen and mirrored images. From the clearly observed objects in the foreground, and from the pensive figure of the barmaid, our eyes move into the reflected background to see, indistinctly, the interior movement of the scene. Impressions of stability in the foreground contrast with the lively background movements.

EDGAR DEGAS

The work of this French artist is widely known and universally admired. His superb draftsmanship, comparable to that of Ingres, whose work you have seen in Plate 40, is immediately apparent. Degas's preoccupation with ballet scenes that often show young dancers practicing, and his keen interest in colorful French horseracing scenes resulted in a large number of fine drawings, paintings, and pastels. Equally interesting in Degas's work is his approach to portraiture. Without losing his keen sense of the personalities he was portraying, he struck a new note of informality and apparent casualness.

Although Degas, like Manet, was an early member of the Impressionist group, he did not wholly accept their theories of painting techniques. For one thing, he was very much concerned with the character, appearance, and activities of people from all walks of life. Then, too, he was a "studio painter," who did not follow the Impressionists in their out-of-doors approach to painting. An inveterate sketcher, he carefully posed his models in his own studio or in other indoor areas. Degas not only experimented with many color media, but he also introduced a pleasant and informal way of arranging figures within his compositions.

The Glass of Absinthe (Plate 43) is, first of all, a striking example of Degas's interest in the passing scenes of Paris. This painting caused a furor and much condemnation when it was first shown in Paris, but it is now considered a highly expressive work of art. The atmosphere of the café, with two lonely figures lost in dismal thoughts, is dramatized by the use of somber grays and browns repeated in various areas of the painting. The scene is abruptly cut off on the right-hand side, very much as a "candid camera" picture might be, yet Degas composed it very carefully, using two friends, an actress and a fellow artist, to impersonate café habitués. We are drawn into the painting through the movement of the zigzag lines that lead our eyes toward the faces of the sad couple. They invite us to contemplate their melancholy lot, or to sympathize with their dejected resignation.

HENRI ROUSSEAU

In contrast to the highly professional work of Ingres, Manet, and Degas, we see in *Baby's Party* (Plate 44) the work of a famous primitive painter. Henri Rousseau was neither a skilled draftsman, a trained painter, nor an outstanding colorist. He was self-taught, beginning as a Sunday painter. Not until he was over forty years of age did he completely give himself over to an overwhelming desire to paint. The directness, sincerity, and childlike quality of his work did not attract the public, but were recognized by important artists of his time.

Rousseau had a unique gift for seeing and presenting his subjects. Here the child, proudly displaying his puppet, dominates the scene. Shapes and colors are arranged in a clear, bold pattern. The simply expressed and unified figure is delightfully contrasted with minutely rendered flowers, foliage, and blades of grass. Repetitions and color movements of reds, blues, yellows, greens, and whites establish an instinctive balance that seems characteristic of the sturdy young subject.

PIERRE-AUGUSTE RENOIR

While Renoir's interest in the effects of light on color was characteristic of the Impressionists, he was not content, as they were, to record only the

PLATE 44. Baby's Party. *Henri Rousseau (French, 1844-1910).*
Oil on canvas. Kunsthaus, Winterthur, Switzerland

PLATE 45. Self-Portrait.
Pierre-Auguste Renoir (French, 1841-1919).
Oil on canvas. Private collection

PLATE 46. Two Girls at the Piano.
Pierre-Auguste Renoir (French,
1841-1919). Oil on canvas.
The Louvre, Paris, France

temporary aspects of his subject. The essential structure of forms in space, as the compositional elements of painting, always engaged him. For this reason, Renoir is known today as the painter who pointed the way toward a new art movement, Post-Impressionism. This is the movement that later on was firmly established by Paul Cézanne, whose paintings you will see later in this chapter. Renoir carried the study of color and light into a style that was completely individual and personal. Small strokes of pure color were used to reproduce the shimmer of light and sunshine. Placed side by side, these colors gave his paintings a vibrant surface quality. Renoir's light touch and airy brush strokes are characteristic of all his work, whether the subject was painted outdoors or indoors.

In Renoir's *Self-Portrait* (Plate 45) we see him at an advanced age, yet still painting with undiminished skill. The portrait reflects the warmth of his personality and his friendly, gentle spirit. The transparency of the colors and their soft textural qualities blend with the sensitive expression of his face. You may have noticed that few self-portraits are painted in a profile view. If Renoir used the mirror technique to make his self-portrait, it is obvious that more than one mirror would be needed to enable him to see his profile. You might find it interesting to see if you could make an arrangement of mirrors that would reflect a view of your profile in such a way that you could draw it.

In *Two Girls at the Piano* (Plate 46) there is sensitive, beautiful draftsmanship and a strong feeling for the structure of the human figure. A haze of caressing colors envelops the whole scene. This painting is a typical example of Renoir's delight in the use of color to express the youth and charm of his models. Typical, also, is his use of two figures, one overlapping the other and so posed as to lead the eyes gently around and into the painting, thus creating a serene, rhythmic opposition of line and color.

The portrait of *Victor Chocquet* (Plate 48) brings out the understanding nature of the man who befriended Renoir and Cézanne when they were being ridiculed by the public and the critics alike. This painting is typical of Renoir's mastery in painting flesh tones. They are subtly varied and give strength and character to the modeling of his subject's face. Paint is applied with varying degrees of richness and mellowness. The hair and beard are blended with equal attention to color and texture. The power of expression emanating from the glowing brown eyes of Victor Chocquet gives the portrait its penetrating expression. In this painting, as in those made later on in his lifetime, Renoir probed deeply into the foundations of drawing and painting, striving always for discipline and structure, as well as for rich and luminous color.

AUGUSTE RODIN

The theories of the Impressionists, introduced by the painters Edouard Manet and Claude Monet, affected many artists of the nineteenth century. Among them was Rodin, the famous French sculptor. Although his work re-

PLATE 47. The Sculptor Jules Dalou. *Auguste Rodin (French, 1840-1917). Bronze. The Rodin Museum, Paris, France*

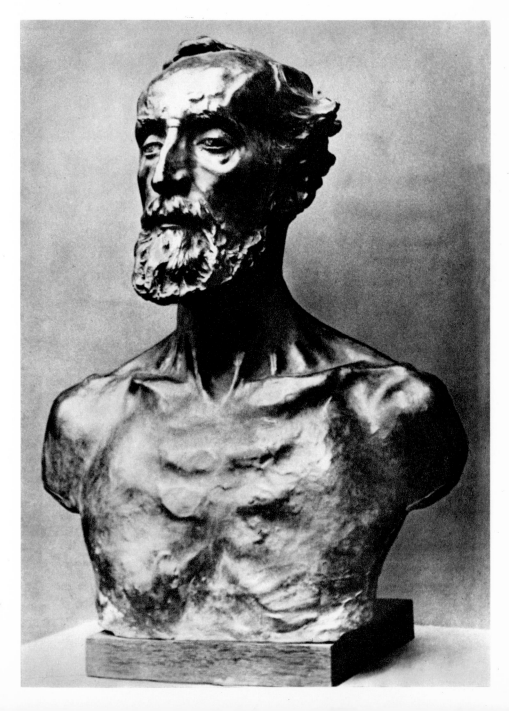

PLATE 48. Victor Chocquet. *Pierre-Auguste Renoir (French, 1841-1919).*
Oil on canvas. Collection Oskar Reinhart, Winterthur, Switzerland

PLATE 49. Victor Chocquet. *Paul Cézanne (French, 1839-1906).*
Oil on canvas. Private collection

tained much of the classical tradition found in Renaissance sculpture, especially that by Michelangelo, Rodin exaggerated the variations of depth in the surfaces of his sculpture, hollowing some areas and building up others. He did this to bring out effects of light and shadow, and to give emphasis and vitality to the forms he created. In looking at *The Sculptor Jules Dalou* (Plate 47) you will note in the almost nervous quality of the head the vitality of the human spirit it represents.

Rodin modeled his subjects in wax or clay. The flexibility of these materials allowed him to use them freely and to give his work a spontaneous and fluid quality, which remained even in the final versions in marble or bronze. If you look back to some of the sculpture that you have seen in the first chapter of this book, you will find that smooth, carefully finished surfaces traditionally are a part of the sculptor's technique. Just as the Impressionist painters rejected smoothly finished surfaces of paint in favor of spontaneous and broken brush strokes, so Rodin discarded what he thought to be a superficial and deadly smoothness that removed his subjects from the living world of light and atmosphere.

PAUL CEZANNE

Cézanne, today called the father of modern painting, definitely established a direction that moved away from the Impressionist style and theory. In comparing his painting *Victor Chocquet* (Plate 49) with Renoir's interpretation of the same subject, one clearly sees the meaning of the new movement known as Post-Impressionism. Cézanne and Renoir both lived in France at the same time, yet each artist had quite a different view of life, of the goals of painting, and of ways in which to achieve them. Renoir's work could never be confused with that of Cézanne, for each artist painted with quite a different intent.

Cézanne's aim was clear: to create a three-dimensional reality, and to do so with a minimum of surface detail. In studying his portrait of Chocquet, we see that the form and planes of the head and face take precedence over all other considerations. Cézanne built this head almost as a sculptor would have done. One is conscious of the solid form created by strong, meaningful strokes of paint. There is no surface blending of colors to soften edges or to harmonize colors, such as may be found in Renoir's painting. Cézanne's color is confined to variations of green and to warm, heavy flesh tones. Because of its limited range, his use of color has great impact. We are led into a new world of seeing, where inner truth is much more important than the beauty of surface effects.

In his *Self-Portrait* (Plate 50) we again see Cézanne's serious, heavy, and searching approach to painting. While the outward appearance of the artist may seem incomplete in many ways, the inner reality of the man speaks out with great force. Cézanne always strove to make his work monumental. The firmness and solidity of his likeness reveals his self-assurance and fearless pioneering spirit. Although many contemporary critics considered his work inept, its revolutionary aspects paved the way for many still newer and even more modern directions in art.

While Cézanne viewed many of his models with great detachment, we have seen in his study of Victor Chocquet that at other times he has become deeply involved in their personalities. In *Old Woman with Rosary* (Plate 51) Cézanne gives us a deeply introspective study of a humble, toil-worn old woman, whose hands tell us as much about her life as her face does. What did the artist see in his model to make such a profound study of her? The very fact that her life was a hard one, that she was bent with care and wore weather-beaten clothing made her the means by which the artist could comment on the hardships and tribulations of life. The irregularity of her features is emphasized by planes of various colors, and the bony structure of her head is revealed through its firm contours. An old peasant cap helps to form a strong unit of the head and face. The folds of the heavy garments, which envelop a body strong in spite of age, are expressive of its solidity. The dark areas around sleeves and hands stress significant forms and are there for that definite purpose. One feels the humility and completely resigned spirit of this woman as expressed in the stiff, worn hands that clasp her prayer beads closely. Cézanne was able to give this painting of a peasant woman an air of grandeur and dignity. He captured a type of beauty that goes deeper than the fresh prettiness of youth.

PLATE 50. Self-Portrait. *Paul Cézanne (French, 1839-1906).*
Oil on canvas. Private collection, Massachusetts

PLATE 51. Old Woman with Rosary. *Paul Cézanne (French, 1839-1906).*
Oil on canvas. The National Gallery, London, England

7

New Pathways in Art

YOU WILL NOW BECOME ACQUAINTED with a number of other painters who, like Cézanne, are known as Post-Impressionists. Working during the late nineteenth and early twentieth centuries, each one brought new dimensions to painting and each is now characterized as a "modern" painter of his time.

GEORGES SEURAT

One of the important artists in the Post-Impressionist group, Georges Seurat, died at the age of thirty-one. Within the short period of nine years, however, he produced a small yet vastly important collection of paintings and a larger number of superb drawings.

Many of these drawings were made in preparation for paintings that he carried out by a meticulous and scientific use of tiny dots of pure, unmixed complementary colors, in a manner that became known as pointillism. All of his drawings reveal Seurat's particular interest in the use of light and shade to produce effects of volume and mass.

The conté-crayon portrait of his friend and fellow student, *Aman-Jean* (Plate 52), shows a greatly simplified head and figure in profile view. Notice how skillfully the light areas have been placed to reveal the model's physical structure and his character. Only the important shapes and planes are stressed. The closeness and richness of light and dark values create a portrait that has a strongly emotional quality.

PAUL GAUGUIN

Another leader in this modern group of highly individual personalities was the French artist Paul Gauguin. Although a wealthy stockbroker, he rejected a conventional and comfortable mode of life in order to devote himself to painting. Initially he worked in Paris; then, with Vincent van Gogh, for a period of time he painted in Arles, in the southern part of France. Gauguin, like other restless painters of this time, began experiments that were later to result in a revolutionary use of color. Shortly after Gauguin's death certain of these artists became known to critics as *Les Fauves*, or wild beasts.

Breton Women (Plate 54) was painted by Gauguin in Brittany when he was struggling to reach a purely personal means of expression. We see his characteristic use of flat areas of color placed against a simplified background, thus creating a strongly patterned design. The broken color and direct brush strokes are reminiscent of his early studies of Impressionism. The poetic mood of *Breton Women* and its richness and subtlety of color remind one of Renoir's paintings.

PLATE 52. Aman-Jean. *Georges Seurat (French, 1859-1891). Conté crayon on paper. The Metropolitan Museum of Art, New York, N.Y. (Bequest of Stephen C. Clark, 1960)*

85

PLATE 53. Self-Portrait. *Paul Gauguin (French, 1848-1903).*
Oil on canvas. Collection Arthur Sachs, Paris, France

PLATE 54. Breton Women. *Paul Gauguin (French, 1848-1903).*
Oil on canvas. The Bavarian State Collection, Munich, Germany

PLATE 55. Tahitian Women. *Paul Gauguin (French, 1848-1903).*
Oil on canvas. Museum of Impressionism, The Louvre, Paris, France

87

Gauguin's characteristic use of flat, brilliant color, and a special quality of design and decoration were soon to become hallmarks of his work. This is apparent in his *Self-Portrait* (Plate 53). Against a background of brilliant red his fur hat and massive shoulders, clad in a blue cloak, form a simple yet brilliant pattern. The dynamic head, with its challenging eyes and angular, bony structure, clearly suggests Gauguin's strength of character.

Gauguin became dissatisfied with life in France and departed for the island of Tahiti in the South Pacific. There he found inspiration in the exotic and colorful life of the natives. These childlike, primitive people seemed to him to be in harmony with the naturally brilliant colors of the earth, sea, and tropical vegetation. Deeply inspired, Gauguin worked incessantly, drawing, painting, and making woodblock prints. The more he painted, the closer his style became related to his surroundings. In *Tahitian Women* (Plate 55) he shows us two earthy, placid figures woven into a colorful and decorative design. The pattern of their strong bodies, silhouetted against sea and sand, draws our attention to the tapestrylike scene. The artist painted the faces of the women in smooth, unbroken planes of color, thus retaining the qualities of simplicity and directness that he so admired.

VINCENT VAN GOGH

Vincent van Gogh, the Dutch artist who worked briefly with Gauguin in southern France, shows us a direction in painting very different from that taken by Gauguin. Each was clearly individual in nature and inclination; so too did each one differ in his manner of work. Van Gogh had also experimented with Impressionism, but what he learned about its theories of broken color he expanded to an extraordinary degree of originality. His intense nature and burning desire to express his feelings about what he saw and painted led to a later movement called Expressionism. Van Gogh did not consciously plan to start or to contribute to the new movement, but he brought the impact of his personality to bear upon all his work to such a degree that he is considered a forerunner of this style. Expressionist painting involves a highly emotional and personal reaction to one's subject. In looking at Van Gogh's paintings, you immediately sense his capacity for personal reaction and expression.

This is particularly evident in his *Self-Portrait* (Plate 56). We are plunged directly into the inner depths of his nature. The brush strokes almost seem to carve the paint into the swirling contours of head and face. One can almost feel him at work, for there is a vital, moving quality in the strange color contrasts and in the piercing expressiveness of the face. Van Gogh's restless, almost tortured manner of painting is a key to the understanding of his personality. His new use of color greatly heightens the effectiveness of all his paintings. Unusual colors for flesh tones range from greens to yellow-oranges; these same colors appear again as violent contrasts in the hair, beard, and hand.

In the portrait of Van Gogh's physician, *Dr. Gachet* (Plate 57), we can sense much of the artist's own suffering and mental turmoil reflected in the strained face of his model. Lines of worry start a continuous, rhythmic movement that leads the observer's eyes around the curved edge of the jacket down to his hand, then moves them over to the book and flowers on the table. Everything that Van Gogh saw is molded by his manner of seeing and feeling into an integral part of the painting. The color is highly symbolic, for the strangely pale colors of face and hands describe a person who was himself ill and who felt an intuitive sympathy for his patient. Yet, even without knowing anything of the personal history of either the artist or his model, one can read a story into the painting, as well as enjoy its unique style.

That a modern and highly individual artist like Van Gogh could learn from an Old Master is understandable only when one knows what the artist is seeking. Van Gogh was a great admirer of his countryman, Rembrandt, and this fact is recorded in his own writings. Turn to the Frontispiece to study again the powerful painting that is characteristic of Rembrandt. When Van Gogh said, "I would be satisfied with a piece of bread the entire day, just to sit before a Rembrandt painting," it was not because he intended to imitate Rembrandt's art. He sought to analyze its source of strength. How did Rembrandt succeed in putting so much life and emotion into his paintings? What was the secret of his magnificent drawing that is neither stiff nor photographic, but possessed with immense inner power? These and many other questions Van Gogh pondered over. In his own work he never lost control of thorough and masterful drawing. Countless studies in chalk, charcoal, and pen-and-ink show the concentration and care he lavished on everything he drew. These subjects ranged from an ordinary pipe, a pair of wooden shoes, and simply made furniture to trees, gardens, houses, and people, all part of the life around him.

In the portrait *Père Tanguy* (Plate 59) Van Gogh shows us the strong bond of sympathy he felt for this old shopkeeper who was kind and helpful

PLATE 56. Self-Portrait. *Vincent van Gogh (Dutch, 1853-1890).*
Oil on canvas. Stedelijk Museum, Amsterdam, Holland

PLATE 57. Dr. Gachet. *Vincent van Gogh (Dutch, 1853-1890).*
Oil on canvas. The Louvre, Paris, France

PLATE 58. Portrait of an Actor. *Sharaku (Japanese, active about 1795).*
Woodcut print in color. Museum of Fine Arts, Boston, Mass.

to him. Every stroke of paint emphasizes the unusually determined drawing
of features and clothing. The figure has been placed in the model's own shop,
where some paintings by Van Gogh are on view. Included are some decorative
Japanese woodblock prints that were very popular at that time. Van Gogh
himself was inspired by the fine design quality of these prints. This painting
shows his admiration of them as well as his warm regard for his subject.

SHARAKU

The art of the colored woodcut print reached its height in Japan during the eighteenth century. An early Chinese invention, it developed from a simple line process into one that involved both artist and skilled printer. Woodcut prints became more than inexpensive book illustrations; they were considered works of art in their own right. Unlike Japanese paintings, they were widely distributed and enjoyed by people in all walks of life.

Sharaku was one of the important Japanese woodcut artists. One of his specialties was portraying actors in dramatic and beautifully designed poses. His *Portrait of an Actor* (Plate 58) reveals the rhythmic lines, the simplicity of shapes, and the restrained but highly effective use of pattern that Manet,. Degas, Van Gogh, and other contemporary artists greatly admired.

AMEDEO MODIGLIANI

This artist was an early twentieth-century Italian painter and sculptor who worked in Paris and, like many of his contemporaries, departed from traditional painting. His *Self-Portrait* (Plate 60) reveals a style of painting totally different from that of Van Gogh. The elongated head and features serve to emphasize the expression and mood he wished to create. Although the artist himself was not a calm and reflective person—quite the opposite, in fact—he has emphasized these qualities in his own portrait. It has, oddly enough, certain characteristics that remind one of early Italian painting, namely clear, simplified contours and a glowing, sensitive color quality. Furthermore, the distortions of natural proportions and simplified structural planes show Modigliani's interest in African sculpture. Whatever the art influences in a given period may be, however, it requires the strong personality of an artist to fuse them into a telling and meaningful art form. Modigliani's personality met this test.

AFRICAN SCULPTURE

From the early twentieth century onward, we find a wide variety of new movements as well as individual styles. This variety resulted from many influences, present and past. You have previously seen an example of

PLATE 59. Père Tanguy. *Vincent van Gogh (Dutch, 1853-1890).*
Oil on canvas. Courtesy M. Knoedler and Co.

PLATE 60. Self-Portrait. *Amedeo Modigliani (Italian, 1884-1920).*
Oil on canvas. Collection Mrs. Yolande Penteado Matarazzo, São Paulo, Brazil

the Japanese prints that focused the artists' attention on clearly stated design qualities. Newly discovered African sculpture also aroused great interest among painters and sculptors. Its unusual, fantastic qualities and its exaggerated proportions and distortions stimulated those artists who were interested in emotional rather than visual expression.

African Mask (Plate 61), from the Ivory Coast, is an elegantly designed piece of sculpture and shares the qualities to be seen in many royal personalities. Masks were produced in many areas of Africa for magical and ceremonial purposes. Although we are conscious of the refined shapes, precise carving, and interesting formalizations of the head, horned headdress, and features, we can feel the presence of a majestic and somewhat awesome personality.

The discovery of African sculpture led also to a general appreciation of the art created by people in other, remote lands. It produced an open-mindedness toward primitive art, as well as toward art produced by other than Western civilizations.

PLATE 61. African Mask. *Youre tribe, Ivory Coast, Africa. Wood. The University Museum of the University of Pennsylvania, Philadelphia, Pa.*

HENRI MATISSE

Although he had not originally planned to be an artist, Matisse, at the age of twenty-two, arrived in Paris to study painting. After a period of conventional, academic training, he became interested in the exciting Impressionist movement. Before long he emerged as the leader of a young and vigorous group of painters. In this group were André Derain, Maurice de Vlaminck, Georges Braque, and Georges Rouault. These were the artists who became known as *Les Fauves,* or wild beasts.

In general, the Fauves were known for certain characteristic approaches to painting. One was their rejection of particular color qualities to suggest form, space, and solidity. Explosive, almost shocking color was substituted for color such as you have seen, for example, in Rembrandt's paintings in Plates 29 and 30, where it was shaded to give light and shadow effects. A second characteristic of Fauve painting, found especially in later work by Matisse, was that of a strong surface pattern of clear color that had a decorative quality.

During the long span of his years as a painter, Henri Matisse retained a visual approach to his subject. *Woman with the Hat* (Plate 62) was painted during the early years of his contact with the revolutionary Fauves. The brilliant color scheme, with its pure, shadowless colors, is derived in part from the Impressionist use of complementary colors. Blues and oranges, reds and greens, violets and yellows produce a lively interplay of colors that, especially when seen from a distance, have an extraordinary sparkle and brilliance.

While Matisse's primary interest in making this painting was to experiment with color that was not limited to the appearances of real life, he conveys, perhaps unconsciously, a certain feeling for the model's personality. She seems willing to submerge herself as a person and to accept the artist's desire to redesign her physical surfaces.

MAURICE DE VLAMINCK

Like Matisse, Vlaminck is considered one of the foremost representatives of Fauvism. He was hearty and vigorous; an instinctive and emotional rather than a reasoned and calculated approach to painting was an innate part of Vlaminck's personality.

Together with Henri Matisse and André Derain, Vlaminck produced

PLATE 62. Woman with the Hat.
Henri Matisse (French, 1869-1954).
Oil on canvas. Collection Mr. and Mrs.
Walter A. Haas, San Francisco, Calif.

PLATE 63. Portrait of Derain.
Maurice de Vlaminck (French, 1876-1958).
Oil on canvas. Private collection,
Paris, France

PLATE 64. The Old King.
Georges Rouault (French, 1871-1958).
Oil on canvas. Museum of Art,
Carnegie Institute, Pittsburgh, Pa.

PLATE 65. The Madwoman.
Chaim Soutine (Lithuanian, 1894-1944).
Oil on canvas. The National Museum
of Western Art, Tokyo, Japan

paintings that were the subject of outraged cries of art critics and the art-viewing public as well. In looking at his *Portrait of Derain* (Plate 63) we may at first glance also experience a feeling of shock. Many of the characteristics to be seen in Matisse's painting are also to be found in Vlaminck's painting of his friend. Brilliant colors are boldly brushed, or laid on with a palette knife, or directly squeezed onto the canvas from the paint tube. Strong contrasts of opposing colors are heightened by equally strong contrasts in lights and darks. No attempt has been made to modify color in order to suggest the underlying forms of the head. The purely arbitrary laying on of color tells us that Vlaminck did not feel obligated to reproduce the physical appearance of his subject. We have seen how effectively Van Gogh developed the use of a similarly free painting technique. We may also note, however, that Van Gogh's technique resulted in an intensity of emotional expression, while that of Vlaminck clearly shows that he was not in the least interested in producing a personal interpretation of his subject.

As an art movement, Fauvism was comparatively short-lived. Its creators and followers turned to other interests and to other means of self-expression. Bridging the late nineteenth and early twentieth centuries as they did, however, the Fauves fired the imagination of other contemporary artists and encouraged their attempts to free themselves from the representation of nature.

GEORGES ROUAULT

Influences of Cézanne's theories of painting, as well as those of the Fauves, are evident in the work of Georges Rouault. An unusually bold application of color and the use of heavy black lines, derived from his experiences in designing stained-glass windows, make this artist's work immediately recognizable. Deep, greenish colors, strongly offset by reddish tones, add to the intense mood that in many ways reflected the artist's temperament. His personal feeling for humanity, its sufferings, poverty, and misery, was a dominating force in his representations of people. One is aware of a deeply religious feeling that is combined with the artist's strong sense of the tragic and pathetic side of life. This may be seen in Rouault's portraits that, unlike those of Matisse and Vlaminck, emphasize through face and figure the unique individuality of his subjects.

The Old King (Plate 64) clarifies the fact that Rouault was less concerned with the outward appearance of his subjects than he was with their emotional, intellectual, or spiritual qualities. We can easily see that Rouault abandoned the idea of a "finished" technique in favor of one that was expressive of the intensity of his own feelings about his subject. Rouault's personal use of color is immediately apparent. Rich, glowing colors, enclosed with powerful black outlines, roughly block out the figure of the old king. He seems to be not so much a king as an ordinary man—although wearing a symbolic crown, he holds a simple flower that might have been found along a wayside. Rouault has forcefully made us aware of the unhappiness and inner suffering of a symbolic figure.

CHAIM SOUTINE

This distinguished painter was one of eleven children in a poverty-stricken family in Lithuania. When he was a young man, already devoted to art, he made his way to Paris to study. Soutine's power and originality were recognized by other young Expressionist painters there, and he became a close friend of Modigliani, whose *Self-Portrait* (Plate 60) you have seen. Soutine was also fortunate in winning a certain amount of acceptance from those dealers and collectors who were becoming interested in modern art.

Soutine's work is clearly characterized by his particular use of color. He applied paint in a dynamic manner comparable to that of Van Gogh, and in an even wider variety of techniques. His solid, rich colors, intensified by animated effects of light, create a strongly theatrical mood.

The Madwoman (Plate 65) conveys the intensity with which the artist related himself to his subject. The tightly contained, withdrawn pose of the unfortunate woman, the revelation of her intense inner world, and her distorted, almost inhuman hands launch a penetrating attack on our eyes and minds. You will notice that Soutine has relied on deep, solid colors relieved by flickering highlights that enliven their surfaces. His characteristic use of color, together with exaggerations, distortions, and omissions of detail, creates a painting that is highly suggestive of the artist's own intense, nervous personality.

8

The New Look

IN TODAY'S TECHNOLOGICAL WORLD, the machine plays such an important part in our lives that one might be led to believe that man could wish for nothing more. Yet the creative spirit clearly persists, and the desire to invent, construct, and express oneself through an enormous variety of new materials and new processes is widely seen and recognized today.

To judge the value of the vast output of art work that is presently being displayed in museums and galleries, old and new, is indeed difficult. We may well ask ourselves: "Is this art?" We may wonder whether contemporary art will continue to attract people or prove to be only a passing fashion. Is it a move on the part of the artist to gain personal publicity, or is it part of the pattern of change that has long distinguished the history of art?

It is evident today that comparatively few artists are interested in people as human beings. There are, however, certain of them who have found new and challenging ways to look at, think about, and interpret their fellow men.

PABLO PICASSO

Of all our present-day artists, Pablo Picasso is probably the best known and most influential. His work is both highly praised and severely criticized. His wide range of styles, his experiments and innovations, have kept his

PLATE 66. The Old Guitarist. *Pablo Picasso*
(Spanish, born 1881). Oil on wood.
The Art Institute of Chicago, Chicago, Ill.
(Helen Birch Bartlett Collection)

PLATE 67. Girl on a Ball.
Pablo Picasso (Spanish, born 1881).
Oil on canvas. The Pushkin Museum,
Moscow, U.S.S.R.

103

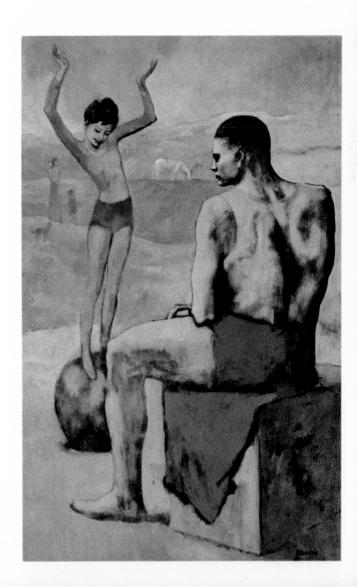

many admirers alert to the almost bewildering variety of ways in which he chooses to express himself.

Although Picasso was born in Spain, he came to live and work in France, where, at an early age, he became one of the most influential artists in the art movements of the twentieth century. Picasso is a living example of an artist who, starting in his youth with the traditional study of realistic art, has worked in a succession of styles. His early works, simple, lively, and somewhat influenced by Impressionism, were replaced by his highly stylized "Blue Period," with its mournful concern for the aged and ill. This phase was succeeded by his interest in circus folk, by his "Rose Period," during which the use of pink and terra-cotta coloring prevailed, then by the influence of African sculpture and by the fundamentally geometric forms that had been the basis of Paul Cézanne's work.

As a result of his study of Cézanne's work, Picasso developed in his painting an entirely new approach to the world of art. He is credited, together with the painter Georges Braque, with being the inventor of Cubism, in which forms are seen by the painter in angular fragments rather than in their totality.

Classical, Surrealistic, and Expressionistic elements later appeared in his work. Throughout his life Pablo Picasso has consistently branched out in unexpected directions, and all his immense art production bears the unmistakable stamp of a highly original personality.

One of the artist's best-known paintings from his Blue Period is *The Old Guitarist* (Plate 66). You may notice, first of all, that we as spectators are very close to the old man and look down on him from a standing position. His emaciated figure almost fills the picture area and is further emphasized by the elongated proportions of the canvas.

The pathetic character of the blind beggar is heightened by the expressive distortion of his figure. Blue, the primary color used, is varied with lighter and darker blues. The color tones of the guitar and the ground are closely related to it. The almost restrictive use of blue establishes the depressed mood both of the subject and of Picasso himself, who at the time that he painted the guitarist was young, poverty-stricken, and as yet unrecognized as an artist.

In *Girl on a Ball* (Plate 67) we have an example of his work when he had emerged from the deep melancholy of his Blue Period and become concerned with the pensive and gentle moods that were a part of the private world of circus acrobats, clowns, and jugglers. This painting shows his manner of simplified and spontaneous drawing. The pose and expression of the figures

PLATE 68. Ambroise Vollard. *Pablo Picasso (Spanish, born 1881).*
Oil on canvas. The Pushkin Museum, Moscow, U.S.S.R.

PLATE 70. Self-Portrait. *Oskar Kokoschka (Austrian, born 1886).*
Oil on canvas. Von der Heydt Museum, Wuppertal, Germany.

are emphasized by elongated lines leading our eyes in a vertical direction. The artist creates a picture of complete concentration in these two sensitively characterized figures. Pink and blue are used sparingly, but the blending and changing of the values of these two colors are sufficient to make this painting seem to have many more colors than it actually has.

The portrait *Ambroise Vollard* (Plate 68) is painted in the Cubist manner. Cubist painters broke up forms and parts of forms into angular shapes that at times became part of the background of the painting. They also saw and painted their subjects from several viewpoints rather than from the single viewpoint of the traditional artist.

In many Cubist paintings it is difficult to connect the work of art with its title because the parts of forms are so broken up and shaded that they seem to dissolve into space. The portrait of Picasso's friend and famous art dealer, Ambroise Vollard, shows us, however, that a convincing portrait can be presented in the Cubist manner. If you partially close your eyes, the face and head emerge, almost as if by magic, from the surface of the painting. The shape and other characteristics of the head and its features strongly suggest a man of great intellectual powers and firm convictions.

In this impressive painting color has been used sparingly. Subdued grays, blues, and browns predominate; contrasting flesh tones have been reserved to center attention upon the model's head and hands.

Portrait of J.R. with Roses (Plate 69) is typical of Picasso's unusual way of reshaping the physical appearance of his model. We notice immediately four characteristics that his work had during the period in which he painted this portrait. Distortion is seen, for example, in the tubular neck. Simplification is easily discovered in the pyramidal shape of the body. Linear movements, as seen in the model's headdress, help the flat planes to suggest solid forms. The multiple view, to be discovered in the profile of the head and the frontal view of the eye, is the fourth characteristic, and one that Picasso used in other paintings to an almost alarming degree.

Once we accept the fact that Picasso, as an artist, is justified in seeing and painting his model with absolute freedom, we can enjoy the extraordinarily strong head with its classical profile; the surface patterns that introduce a lively note; and the casually placed roses that enliven the striking blue background.

Our concepts of art have been greatly broadened in recent years. The initial shock at the sight of daring innovations, such as we have just discovered in Picasso's work, has been tempered by our recognition that art can go far beyond the view of life that we normally see. We now accept the fact that it can, and does, deal with life's internal and even subconscious elements.

OSKAR KOKOSCHKA

The intent to suggest the emotional essence of their subjects, rather than the outward appearance, became the aim of several artists in Central Europe. They formed the spearhead of an art movement that became known as Expressionism, and their work influenced the artists of many countries.

An Austrian by birth, Kokoschka is a leading member of the Expressionist group. He did not experiment in various styles of painting, as many of his fellow artists did; his work from the first showed what we think of today as Expressionistic tendencies. As a young artist he was instinctively concerned with revealing the emotional experiences of his subjects. Through changing and distorting natural appearances of forms and colors, he and other Expressionist painters tried to evoke the inner nature of their subjects.

Kokoschka's *Self-Portrait* (Plate 70) is a telling presentation of his own state of mind. We can sense his reflective and intellectual qualities, as well as the emotional uncertainty under which he labored at the particular time that he was moved to paint this self-portrait, one of several that he made. The ravages of war that left him in mental and physical ill-health are reflected in his countenance and pose. The burning, nervous energy of this visionary painter is clearly revealed by the vibrant quality of his brush strokes and by the active movement of his color treatment.

MARC CHAGALL

Born in Russia long before the revolution there, Chagall as a young man arrived in France and became a part of the group known as the School of Paris. At that time, art was in ferment. Expressionism, Fauvism, Cubism, and early forms of Surrealism all had their leaders, with many artists moving freely from one to another of these manners of art expression.

In the work of Chagall one finds influences of a number of these new art movements. Yet in his painting there is a unique quality: a highly developed poetic imagination and a deep involvement with the world of fantasy. Many of Chagall's paintings have their source in his childhood memories of the

PLATE 71. Self-Portrait with Seven Fingers. *Marc Chagall (Russian, born 1887). Oil on canvas. Stedelijk Museum, Amsterdam, Holland*

PLATE 72. Woman in Native Costume. *Paul Klee (Swiss-German, 1879-1940). Gouache. The Klee Foundation, Berne, Switzerland*

small Russian village where he had lived. Both its realities and its inherited folklore have been retained in the artist's conscious and subconscious mind. Thus it is the irrational rather than the logical elements that impress us most in his paintings.

Self-Portrait with Seven Fingers (Plate 71) shows how freely Chagall moves away from reality. Shapes are simplified and altered; they move about freely. They are bent, twisted, and turned in any direction that pleases the artist. Just as he has presented himself in a happy, lighthearted way, so he has included childlike conceptions of an imaginary world. In this world, as you will notice in the painting on the easel, a cow may be higher than a steeple, and a human being may float through the world at will.

The painter's palette shows an array of all the colors that Chagall used in his self-portrait. They are delightfully brilliant, strangely combined, and used in unexpected places. Since everything in this painting consistently rejects reality, we can easily accept the seven-fingered artist's vision of his fantastic inner world, one that is far removed from actual time and place.

PAUL KLEE

Klee, a Swiss-German artist, as a young man distrusted modern painting, comparing it unfavorably with the work of traditional artists. As he matured, however, he became one of the foremost modernists. His influence on contemporary painting has been widespread, and his writings on art have been extensively studied.

Leaving his native Switzerland at the age of nineteen, Klee studied and worked in Munich and Paris. Although attracted to the work of Cubist painters, particularly to that of Picasso, he gradually found his own, unique means of expression. While certain aspects of Cubism appear in Klee's work, there are also the distinguishing elements of free invention that are based on his highly personal interpretation of the inner life and meaning of his subjects.

Woman in Native Costume (Plate 72) has certain similarities to Picasso's *Portrait of J.R. with Roses* (Plate 69). The heads and figures of both women have been reduced to simple, flat geometric planes. The colors in each painting are restricted and certainly unrelated to the actual appearance of the subjects. Because *Woman in Native Costume* certainly cannot be thought of as a portrait in the usual sense, it is important that we consider its psychological aspects. The ghostly head, with its strange suggestions of both a full front

PLATE 73. The Family. *Marisol Escobar (Venezuelan, born 1930).*
Painted wood and other materials in three sections. The Museum of Modern
Art, New York, N.Y. (Advisory Committee Fund)

and a profile view, challenges our imagination. Its strange, unworldly quality suggests an apparition that is more felt than seen.

MARISOL

Although of Venezuelan parentage, Marisol Escobar, or just Marisol, as she chooses to be called, is a challenging part of the young art world in Paris and New York. Her sculpture is apt to startle people, since it is very different from that to which they are accustomed. *The Family* (Plate 73), for example, is a combination of sculpture, painting, and everyday objects. She has explained that the idea for the group came from a discarded family snapshot. By examining the actual construction of the scene, you will notice a series of wooden panels that include an old door and other flat areas on which much of the five figures has been painted. There are, however, sculptured parts, such as the head of the mother and her baby, as well as constructed parts that project some of the figures toward the observer. While wood is the chief material used, there are additions that have a lifelike quality, such as the mother's carefully modeled hands and real shoes.

The mother's figure has great dignity; she and the baby dominate the scene. In a strong contrast of interpretation and mood, the three children appear very much as we might have observed them posing self-consciously for a photograph.

❊   ❊   ❊

A look back at the past is easier than a look ahead into the unknown future. Thus we can speak of perspective, or the view across a distance, in a figurative way, for it helps us recognize not only the span of time and space, but also the deeds and products of mankind over the centuries. We all learn from history, or hope to do so, and we can gain through further study of the finest examples of man's creative spirit. It is quite another matter to examine today's art scene and to place present-day products in their proper relation to the long history of art that has preceded them. To judge the value of the art of our times, especially that created by artists not too much older than many of you are, is difficult. Time alone will prove what falls into disfavor and what will endure. Yet your personal opinions are very important, for strong convictions about art can contribute to the cultural growth of the world in which we live.

LIST OF ARTISTS

Van der Weyden, Rogier, 32; *Plate 18*

CEZANNE, Paul (*say*-ZAHN)
French, 1839–1906

CHAGALL, Marc (*shah*-GAHL)
Russian, works in France, born 1887

CHARDIN, Jean-Baptiste (*shar*-DAN)
French, 1699–1779

CLOUET, Jean (*kloo*-WAY)
French, 1486?–1541

CRANACH the Elder, Lucas (KRAH-*nak*)
German, 1472–1553

DEGAS, Edgar (*duh*-GAH)
French, 1834–1917

DERAIN, André (*duh*-RAN)
French, 1880–1954

DUCCIO DI BUONINSEGNA (DOO-*cho-dee*
BWO-*nin*-SAY-*nya*)
Italian, 1255?–1319?

DÜRER, Albrecht (DYU-*rer*)
German, 1471–1528

EL GRECO (*el* GRECK-*o*)
Born in Crete, worked in Spain,
1541–1614

GAUGUIN, Paul (*go*-GAN)
French, 1848–1903

GIOTTO (JAWT-*toh*)
Italian, 1266?–1337

GOYA, Francisco (GO-*yah*)
Spanish, 1746–1828

HALS, Frans (HAHLS)
Dutch, 1580–1666

HOGARTH, William (HO-*garth*)
English, 1697–1764

HOLBEIN the Younger, Hans
(HOLE-*bine*) German, 1497–1543

INGRES, Jean-Auguste-Dominique
(ANGR) French, 1780–1867

KLEE, Paul (KLAY)
Swiss-German, 1879–1940

KOKOSCHKA, Oskar (*ko*-KOSH-*ka*)
Austrian, born 1886

LEONARDO DA VINCI (*lay-oh*-NAR-*doh*
dah VEEN-*chee*) Italian, 1452–1519

MANET, Edouard (*ma*-NAY)
French, 1832–1883

MARISOL [Escobar] (MA-*ri-sol*)
Born in Venezuela, 1930,
works in USA

MATISSE, Henri (*ma*-TEECE)
French, 1869–1954

MICHELANGELO BUONARROTI (*mick-el-*
AHN-*jel-oh*) Italian, 1475–1564

MODIGLIANI, Amedeo (*moh-dil-*
YAH-*ni*) Italian, worked in France,
1884–1920

MONET, Claude (*moh*-NAY)
French, 1840–1926

PERUGINO [Pietro Vannucci]
(*pe-ru*-GEE-*no*) Italian, 1446?–1523

PHIDIAS (FI-*di-yus*)
Greek, c. 450 B.C.

PICASSO, Pablo (*pi*-CAH-*so*)
Spanish, works in France,
born 1881

RAPHAEL SANZIO (RA-*fi-el*)
Italian, 1483–1520

REMBRANDT VAN RIJN (REM-*brant*
van RINE) Dutch, 1606–1669

RENOIR, Pierre-Auguste (*renn*-WAHR)
French, 1841–1919

RODIN, Auguste (*ro*-DAN)
French, 1840–1917

ROUAULT, Georges (*roo*-OH)
French, 1871–1958

ROUSSEAU, Henri (*roo*-SO)
French, 1844–1910

RUBENS, Peter Paul (ROO-*bens*)
Flemish, 1577–1640

SEURAT, Georges (*ser*-AH)
French, 1859–1891

SHARAKU (SHAR-*ra-koo*)
Japanese, active c. 1795

SOUTINE, Chaim (*soo*-TEEN)
Russian, worked in France,
1894–1944

STUART, Gilbert
American, 1755–1828

TITIAN (TISH-*un*)
Italian, 1477? (more probably
c. 1490)–1576

VAN EYCK, Jan (*van* AIK)
Flemish, 1370?–1441

VAN GOGH, Vincent (*van* GOK or
van GO) Dutch, worked in France,
1853–1890

VASARI, Giorgio (*vah*-ZAR-*i*)
Italian, 1511–1574

VELÁZQUEZ, Diego (*ve*-LASS-*kes* or
bay-LATH-*keth*) Spanish, 1599–1660

VERMEER, Jan (*vair*-MARE)
Dutch, 1632–1675

VERROCCHIO, Andrea del (*ve*-ROH-
kee-oh) Italian, 1435–1488

VLAMINCK, Maurice de (*vla*-MANK)
French, 1876–1958

WEYDEN, Rogier van der (VAN *der*
VAI-*den*) Flemish, 1400?–1464

GLOSSARY

ACADEMIC   Any style or movement following established rules and precepts of the leading art academies in particular periods.

A.D.   Abbreviation for *Anno Domini* (the year of the Lord). Signifies the calendar of the Christian era, dating from the year 1 onward.

AESTHETIC   As used in this book, pertaining to the science and study of beauty in art.

AFRICAN ART   African Negro art comes chiefly from the central part of Africa, extending from the west coast into the interior. Known to Europeans in the fifteenth century, African sculpture was brought to Europe in large quantities in the late nineteenth century and aroused great interest and attention. Ancestor and nature worship are important among the basic factors in shaping the styles of African art. Little is known of the early history of this art.

BAROQUE   A seventeenth-century European style, characterized by bold and twisting line movements with emphasis on strong action. Complicated, often fantastic figures are typical of Baroque painting.

B.C.   Abbreviation for *Before Christ*, dating the era of prehistoric times from earliest known records and counting down to the year 1 of the Christian era.

CARTOON   A full-size design or study to be used as the model for a painting, tapestry, mosaic, or stained-glass window. Cartoon in the sense of "funny picture" developed from this term.

CHINESE ART   Dates from the Neolithic period, about 3000 B.C. The art of a vast territory that includes Tibet, Mongolia, and Korea with all of China is often included in this term.

CLASSIC   Describes stylistic standards that include restraint, simplicity, harmony, and the search for ideal proportions. The fifth century B.C. in Greece is considered the finest period of Classic art.

COLOR   This word may be divided into several categories: *Hue* is the actual color as we know it. Primary hues in painting include red, yellow, blue; secondary hues are orange, green, and violet; and intermediary hues are made through mixing. *Value* refers to the lightness or darkness of hues, and may also refer to black, white, and grays. *Intensity* refers to degrees of brightness or dullness of color. *Color schemes* are the combination or arrangement of varying types of colors: neighboring, analogous (corresponding), or related, and opposing or contrasting colors. There are certain descriptive terms that pertain to color: *monochromatic,* or varying tones of one hue; *warm* (reds and yellows) and *cool* (blues and blue-greens); *advancing* and *receding,* the power of color to produce effects of space, volume, and depth; *opaque* and *transparent,* the quality of light penetration.

COMPOSITION   An arrangement or grouping of all elements within a large design or a selected area.

CONVENTIONAL   A way of representing subjects, objects, and figures according to fixed rules often dictated by an earlier tradition. Sometimes used to suggest lack of imagination.

CRAFTSMAN   A skilled worker who produces handwork of superior quality as a result of his mastery of tools and techniques.

CUBISM   An art movement starting about 1907, in which the chief aim was to render the visible world in terms of simplified geometric forms—cubes, cones, and rectangular planes—in whole or in part, and from many viewpoints.

DESIGN   A planned arrangement of lines, shapes, forms, textures, and colors.

DISTORTION   A rearrangement or an exaggeration of the normal sizes, proportions, and shapes of familiar forms for the purpose of giving them greater emotional or dramatic meaning or impact.

DRAFTSMAN   An artist who draws with precision and power. Also used in the fields of architecture and other forms of construction to denote the person who draws plans according to exact specifications.

DRAWING   A term that may describe either a process or a product. Representation of what the artist sees, feels, or thinks about, on a two-dimensional surface, usually paper. Materials used include pencil, silverpoint on specially coated paper, pen and ink, brush and ink, charcoal, and various types of crayon, such as lithographic and conté crayon.

EXPRESSIONISM   A twentieth-century style of painting characterized by free distortion of form and color for the expression of intense personal emotions and inner sensations.

FAUVISM   An art movement of the early twentieth century, developed in France and characterized by unconventional arrangements, bold strokes, and strong colors often applied straight out of the tube.

FORM   In painting, form refers to three-dimensional effects produced either by structural drawing or by surfaces that suggest depth and solidity. In sculpture, refers to *free forms* (original forms deviating from natural or geometric forms), *closed forms* (solid masses); *open forms* (spaces that penetrate masses). Other descriptive words applied to qualities of form are: basic, geometric, simplified, functional, expressive, complex.

FORMAL   Following set rules and standards. Emphasis is on symmetry of composition, regularity of forms and spaces, simplified color, smooth finishes.

FRESCO   Mural painting in watercolor on plaster walls that are especially prepared and still moist during the painting process.

GOUACHE   Now sometimes called tempera. The pigment is mixed with water, and thickened with gum arabic to make the color opaque.

GREEK ART   The total period extends from about 1100 B.C. to 150 B.C. First is the *Geometric* style, until 600 B.C.; it is followed by the *Archaic* style, until 500 B.C.; *Early Classic* art, until 450 B.C.; *Classic* art, which extends to 323 B.C. The last phase of Greek art is called the *Hellenistic* style, which blends with Roman art.

IMPRESSIONISM   A style of painting developed in the second half of the nineteenth century. French artists developed a method for recording the fleeting effects of light and atmosphere, using small strokes or touches of color. The technique was intended to let the observer's eye "blend" the colors, thus creating a greater sense of luminosity than if the artist mixed the colors in his palette.

LINE   As used in drawing or painting, refers to the real or imaginary edges or outlines of objects, forms, or spaces. *Contour lines* specifically describe the outer edges of forms. *Line direction* means the total movement of spaces or forms as seen in works of art. Qualities of line may be delicate or forceful, precise or vague, soft or hard, static or active, rhythmic or chaotic, flowing or jerky.

MOSAIC   A technique in which small pieces of colored glass, stone, or other materials are inlaid in an adhesive background material to form a pattern; also, the decorations made by this process.

MURAL   A large wall painting made either directly on the surface of a wall (see FRESCO) or on canvas attached permanently to a wall. The term may also refer to other types of wall decoration, such as those that are inlaid or carved.

PAINTING   The art of using a fluid medium for decoration of a flat surface, usually of canvas, wood, or plaster. Watercolor, oil, tempera, and synthetic paints are commonly used. Paintings may express all possible qualities of depth, atmosphere, space, form, and movement through the use of color.

PERSPECTIVE   The technique of representing on a flat surface the position in space of objects as they appear to the eye. *Linear perspective* is based on the fact that receding parallel lines appear to converge on a single vanishing point. There may be many such vanishing points in a single painting. *Atmospheric* or *aerial perspective* suggests depth by diminishing the clarity and color of objects as they are increasingly distant from the eye.

PORTRAIT   A representation of a person—especially of the face—in painting, drawing, sculpture, or photography.

POST-IMPRESSIONISM   A term used to describe the style of French painting following Impressionism. In contrast to Impressionism, it emphasizes form, solidity, and structure, while still preserving the color qualities of Impressionism.

PRINTMAKING   Includes techniques of woodcut and wood engraving, metal plate engraving and etching, and lithography. From the wood block, metal plate, or stone, respectively, the printer can make impressions (prints).

REALISM   In art, the rendering of true-to-life, visible appearances.

RENAISSANCE   Literally, the word means rebirth. The term refers to the discovery, enjoyment, and use of Classical culture and the beginnings of the modern scientific attitude. It dates from the fourteenth to the early sixteenth century in Italy, and slightly later north of the Alps.

RHYTHM   A term used to describe the orderly repetition of lines, tones, colors, and patterns. Rhythm may be extremely obvious and plain, or extremely subtle and complicated.

ROMANTICISM   An early nineteenth-century movement that emphasized highly imaginative, emotional, and storytelling themes, often from history, literature, or faraway places.

SCULPTURE   The art of producing figures or objects in a sculptural medium. *Sculpture in the round* stands free and can be viewed from all sides. *Relief sculpture* remains attached to a surface. *High relief sculpture* is deeply carved. *Low relief* (or *bas-relief*) sculpture has shallow cutting. Sculpture may be carved in stone or wood, or modeled in clay, wax, or plaster. The latter kinds are made permanent by firing, or by casting in a metal, often bronze.

STYLE   Term used to describe the particular qualities and manner of expression which identify a work of art with a period of history or with a group of artists who work in a like manner.

SURREALISM   A twentieth-century style of painting in which the world of dreams and dreamlike fantasy is presented in a lifelike manner and made to seem real. Surrealism "goes beyond" Realism.

TEMPERA   Pigment mixed with egg, sometimes the white, sometimes the yolk, to make an opaque medium. Also see GOUACHE.

TRADITION   Rules or methods of producing art that have been passed along from one generation to another. Some elements of tradition prove useful, workable, and valuable; unthinking use of tradition leads to convention and, at worst, mere imitation.

INDEX

123